Department of the Environment

The Landlord and Tenant Act 1987: Awareness, Experience and Impact

Andrew Thomas
Cathy North
Liz Spencer
Kit Ward

A report of a qualitative study carried out by Social and Community Planning Research on behalf of the Department of the Environment May 1991.

London: HMSO

ISBN 0 11 752458 9

Contents

Acknowledgements

This study was commissioned and funded by the Department of the Environment (DoE) and carried out by a team of researchers from Social and Community Planning Research (SCPR).

We would like to thank all of the tenants, managing agents, landlords, solicitors, housing advisors and housing organisations for taking part in the study. Particular thanks are due to the local authority officers in our study areas for providing information about their housing stock, and Michelle Burrell and Heather Johnson (Camden Federation of Private Tenants) and Gerry Fox (Fineman Lever) for their advice and assistance at the outset of the study.

Summary of Main Findings

Design and coverage of the study

1. A qualitative study was carried out in order to investigate the impact of the provisions of the Landlord and Tenant Act 1987 on the resolution of problems arising from the management of leasehold flats. The study was commissioned by the Department of the Environment and carried out by Social and Community Planning Research.

2. The research was carried out using a combination of group discussions and in-depth exploratory interviews. A total of 131 respondents took part in the study. The study was designed to cover a wide range of people associated with the management of leasehold properties: tenants (95), landlords (10), managing agents (10), housing advisors (10), and solicitors (6).

Sample profile

3. Tenants were selected to provide a broad spread of properties and types of tenure. Of the 95 tenants in the study, 27 rented their accommodation and 68 had bought a lease. Twenty respondents lived in mansion blocks, 28 in newer purpose-built blocks of flats, and 47 in converted houses.

A wide range of managing agents and landlords were included in the study representing a broad spread of property portfolios. Most of the managing agents specialised in residential management. Most of the landlords held the freeholds to properties as a form of capital investment; a small number were builders or property developers whose primary wish was to sell on the freeholds once the building work was complete.

The majority of tenants lived in buildings that were managed by managing agents (39); some were managed by the landlord directly (19); others by management companies owned by the residents themselves (23).

4. Many of the tenants interviewed had experienced some form of problem with the management of their block of flats. Problems generally fell into one of seven categories:

- **Repairs** (e.g. repairs not carried out; poor quality work)

- **Refurbishment** (e.g. too little work carried out; excessive works carried out)

- **Costs** (e.g. cost overruns; estimates 'rigged' by landlords/managing agent; 'unrealistically' high prices charged)

- **Consultation** (e.g. refusal to consult tenants or their observations ignored)

- **Services** (e.g. not provided although specified in lease; services charged for but not provided)

- **Accounting** (e.g. difficulty in obtaining accounts; complex accounts; errors in accounting)

- **Insurance** (e.g. refusal to provide insurance details; landlord keeps money from insurance claims)

Awareness of rights and duties under the 1987 Act

5. Overall, there was a marked lack of awareness of the Landlord and Tenant Act 1987 and its provisions and implications.

6. Tenants were the least well informed, managing agents the most comprehensively informed. A number of landlords were not aware of their duties under the Act; some were not complying through ignorance on their part, others were in compliance but only because their practices happened to be in accord with the Act's provisions rather than through any vigilance on their part.

7. Although the Act applies to management companies run by tenants in the same way as it does to managing agents and landlords, it was notable that, in general, markedly little awareness of the Act's provisions was shown by this group of respondents.

Views about the provisions of the Landlord and Tenant Act 1987

8. Many people viewed the principle of the legislation in a favourable light. They felt that it provided tenants with useful rights whilst maintaining a reasonably equitable balance between the interests of leaseholders and their landlords. However, based on their experiences of using the legislation many respondents felt that the Act was deficient in a number of areas. A summary of the major deficiences is provided below.

- *Information about the landlord*

  Potentially ineffective and easy to evade, with insufficient legal redress and financial penalty for non-compliance.

- *Service charges*

  The process of consultation and the provision within the Act to challenge service charges were generally felt to be ineffectual. The Act was often said to be *"powerless"* to deal with problems of insufficient, inadequate or poor quality management services. In some instances building work and services were said to be carried out to an 'excessive' extent - this too was thought to be inadequately addressed by the 1987 legislation.

- *Consultation over building works*

  While the consultation process, in principle, was viewed very favourably, many felt that the provisions were seriously flawed - the process was felt to have been insufficiently defined and open to interpretation. The lack of legal redress under the 1987 Act for poor quality work, after it had been carried out, was felt to be a major omission.

- *Insurance of the property*

  The ability to challenge the landlord's choice of insurance was often considered to be ineffective with insufficient legal redress where landlords refused to supply copies of the insurance documents.

- *Variation of leases*

  This was generally considered to be a useful provision although the range of conditions under which a deed of variation can be applied for was considered to be too restrictive.

- *Appointment of a manager by the court*

  The process of appointing a manager was generally considered to be lengthy, costly and operable only in a restricted range of circumstances. For example, the provision was felt to operate only in situations where managing agents and landlords were carrying out too little work - situations where excessive services were being provided and charged for were felt to be insufficiently covered by the legislation.

- *Compulsory acquisition*

  The requirement that a management order has to have been operative for three years before proceedings can commence for compulsory acquisition was considered by some, to be excessive. Procedures were also felt to be lengthy and costly which were thought likely to deter its use.

- *Right of first refusal*

  Part I of the Act was generally viewed very favourably. However, two main problems emerged. First, the time periods specified in the legislation were felt to be too short to successfully complete the purchase of the freehold, particularly where large numbers of leaseholders are involved. Second, many respondents felt that leaseholders should be able to purchase the freehold to their own flat - the requirement of collective purchase was felt to be excessivley burdensome. In addition, financial penalties were called for in instances where landlords had evaded, or attempted to evade the law.

Factors limiting the effectiveness of the Landlord and Tenant Act 1987

9. While there is a general view from all parties that the Act has much to commend it, in principle at least, its effectiveness in practice is seriously impaired. Indeed, many respondents felt that while the 1987 Act gave every appearance of conferring rights, in practice the legislation was sufficiently vague for people's rights, in some cases, to become unenforceable. This is primarily for four reasons.

- The Act is felt to have a number of procedural deficiencies and lacks sufficient powers to enforce compliance with the Act's provisions.

- The legislation includes a number of 'grey areas', some of which are specific to individual parts of the Act, others operating throughout the Act. The use of vague and undefined terms are included in this category. The majority of these are related to the use of words and phrases such as 'consult', 'challenge', 'take note of', 'observation' and 'reasonable' which were thought by many respondents to be vague and open to interpretation.

- Landlords and managing agents were said to use a range of 'sharp practices'. Some of these are used to circumvent the law, others are intended to stop or reduce the likelihood of tenants taking legal action.

- The Act includes a small number of loopholes including three which allow freeholders to evade conferring the right of first refusal (Part I).

A large number of examples of these problems are to be found in the main body of the report.

Leaseholding and related management issues

10. In addition to the problems identified with the implementation of the provisions of the 1987 Act, there are also a number of issues that are extraneous to the Act but impinge on the process of using the legislation:

Four primary issues arise.

- Tenants rarely have a full understanding of the concept of 'leasehold' and its implications. Leases are also written in such a way as to give rise to difficulties with implementation and interpretation. The effect of this is, in some cases, to raise the expectations on the part of leaseholders as to the nature of the landlord's duties. It also allows unscrupulous managing agents and landlords to evade their duties.

- Where respondents wished to take action against the managing agent or landlord most found it difficult to ascertain their rights. A considerable need for information about a person's rights and duties under current housing legislation was identified.

- While some people had considered the option of taking court action to resolve a dispute, there was a considerable body of opinion that indicated that this was not the most appropriate way of solving problems. While tenants were reluctant to take legal action for a number of reasons, the issue of cost was the primary reason for not pursuing this course of action.

- There was a general view, primarily from tenants and advisors, that some of the disputes that arise over leasehold management occur because the property management profession practices without formal guidelines or controls. The issue of how management fees are calculated was a particularly salient issue. There was a considerable body of opinion, from all parties, that indicated that property management should be regulated or controlled in some way.

Chapter 1   Introduction

1.1 Background

Under the chairmanship of Mr Edward Nugee, Q. C., the Committee of enquiry on the management of privately owned blocks of flats chronicled a number of problems for tenants concerning the management of the blocks by landlords and managing agents. The inquiry found that often there were excessive delays in the carrying out of maintenance work or repairs, the levels of service charges did not always reflect the quality of the service provided, tenants were not consulted over the work that was done, and, overall the general dissemination of information to tenants, by landlords, was poor. Additionally the committee of inquiry identified two further problems: the landlords' identity might not be known or the landlord might not be based in this country, and the existence of poorly drafted leases giving rise to difficulties in their implementation.

The Landlord and Tenant Act 1987, which was based almost entirely on the proposals of the Nugee Committee, seeks to remedy these deficiencies. This is done by strengthening the rights of tenants in a number of ways. For example, a role in the management of the property by way of consultation over repairs and improvements; the ability to apply to court for a variation of the lease, and the right to certain information. The Act also gives tenants the right to apply to court for the appointment of a manager if the landlord or agent are not managing the building properly; and in extreme cases, the compulsory acquisition of the landlord's interest in the block. Where the landlord wishes to sell the property, tenants are given the right of first refusal which enables them to negotiate collectively for its purchase.

The provisions of the Landlord and Tenant Act 1987 were introduced in stages over the period February 1988 to April 1989. The commencement dates for each part of the Act are shown in Appendix A.

In order to assess the general awareness and potential impact of the Landlord and Tenant Act 1987, the Department of the Environment commissioned Social and Community Planning Research to undertake a research study. This report documents the findings of that research, which was carried out between July 1990 and February 1991.

1.2 The Landlord and Tenant Act 1987 and its relationship to other legislation

With the 'break up' of older privately rented blocks of flats for owner occupation and the growth in new leasehold flat building and conversion, a series of legislative changes were introduced from the 1970s onwards that were designed to cope with the increasing number of management problems that were occurring. For example:

Section 90 of the Housing Finance Act 1972 gave leaseholders the right to be shown how their service charges were calculated.

Sections 121 and 122 of the Housing Act 1974 required the landlord to disclose their identity to leaseholders and, on request, inform them of the identity of the new landlord following a disposal of the property.

In addition to repeating the right to information about service charge calculations, the Housing Act 1980 (section 136 and schedule 19) enabled the leaseholders to challenge them in court as being unreasonable.

The 1985 Landlord and Tenant Act repeated the provisions of the earlier legislation but stopped short of providing powers to minimise the likelihood of problems arising from the day to day management of leasehold properties.

The Landlord and Tenant Act 1987 was designed to redress these problems by specifying the rights of leaseholders and the duties of landlords.

The Landlord and Tenant Act 1987
Management of leasehold property

The 1987 Act includes a number of management provisions. For example, to ensure that any service charges paid by the tenants are available for the purpose for which they were collected and not liable to be lost should the landlord become insolvent, the Act provides for service charges to be held in trust by the landlord. In addition, recognised tenants associations have the right to be consulted when the landlord is considering the appointment of an agent to manage the property. Tenants also have the right to inspect the property insurance and can ask landlords to provide a written summary.

Information

In order to exercise their rights, tenants need to know their landlord's name and address. While it is already an offence under the Landlord and Tenant Act 1985 for landlords to withhold this information, until the 1987 Act came into force there was no injunction available to compel the landlord to do this. Part VI of the Act requires that the landlord's name and address must be stated on any written rent or service charge demand and if that address is not in England and Wales an address in England and Wales at which notices can be served must be provided. Where the landlord's name and address are not supplied, tenants have the right to withhold payment of service charges until this is complied with. Additionally, the tenant is given the right, where the land is registered, to obtain the landlords' name from the Land Register.

Variation of Leases

The Act provides for tenants of a lease of more than 21 years to apply to the court to collectively have aspects of the lease changed, where the provisions of the lease relating to the repair and maintenance of the property, insurance and service charges are unsatisfactory. This part of the Act is intended to apply to leases which are so badly defective that they could not be regarded as providing adequately for the proper maintenance and care of the block, the well being of the leaseholder and the legitimate interest of the landlord. Where not all parties are agreeable the Act makes provision for the majority of qualifying long leaseholders to support the application: for example, where the application is made in respect of nine or more leases, at least 75% of qualifying tenants must support the application and not more than 10% can oppose it.

Appointment of managers by the court

Where landlords fail to carry out their legal obligations, Section 37 of the Supreme Court Act 1981 gives the High Court the power to appoint a receiver to take over the management functions for a property. The Nugee Committee felt that this legislation, which remains unaffected by the 1987 Act, should only be used as a last resort for urgent matters. Tenants of a flat, except business tenants, now have the right to apply to the County or High Courts for the appointment of a person to perform the functions of a manager where the landlord fails to carry their legal obligations (specified in the lease or implied by existing statutes) for example, in terms of repairs and maintenance. Under the 1987 Act the procedures required for the appointment of a manager are less formal, but do require that tenants serve notice on the landlord of their decision to go to court, specify the grounds on which the application to court is made, and give landlords 'reasonable' time in which to put matters right. Courts may only make an order to appoint a manager where there is a breach by the landlord of their management obligations and these are likely to continue.

Compulsory acquisition by tenants of their landlord's interest in the property

Part III of the Act allows tenants to go further than appointing a manager, and in certain circumstances, allows them to apply to the courts to compulsory acquire their landlord's interest in the property. In order to use this part of the Act a majority of 'qualifying' tenants must approve the court application, who, for the purposes of this part of the Act, are tenants who hold a lease to a flat of at least 21 years, and who are not business tenants. A notice must be served on the landlord, stating the grounds for the court application for compulsory purchase, and provide the landlord an opportunity to remedy the complaint. There are two grounds for the court to make an order to compulsory acquire the property. First, as with Part II of the Act (Appointment of managers by the court) the landlord must be in breach of their management obligations, but in this instance the breach must be likely to continue and to be a situation in which the appointment of a manager under Part II of the Act would not be an adequate remedy. Second, the premises should have been subject to a management order under Part II of the Act for the previous three years.

Tenants' rights of first refusal

The Act gives qualifying tenants the right of first refusal if the landlord intends to sell or dispose of the property. The Act applies to properties where more than 50% of the flats are held by 'qualifying tenants'. Qualifying tenants include all tenants of flats, except protected shorthold tenants, business tenants, tenants whose tenancy is terminable on cessation of employment, or those tenants who have a tenancy covering more than half the number of flats contained in the building, or whose tenancy extends to more than one flat or any common parts of the property. Where tenants are offered the landlord's interest in the property, the offer must remain open for at least two months. In order to accept it more than half of the tenants must be in agreement - at least 90% of the qualifying tenants must be 'served notice' of the landlord's intention to dispose of the property. Where tenants accept the landlord's offer, the landlord may not sell for three months to anyone but the person or persons nominated by the tenants. If the tenants do not wish to purchase the property, then the landlord can dispose of the property to any other person, though not at a price lower than that offered to the tenants. Where these provisions are not complied with the Act enables the tenants to compulsorily purchase the property from the new landlord.

1.3 Aims and scope of the study

The central objective of the research was to investigate the impact of these provisions in the resolution of problems arising from the management of properties. Within this main requirement, the study had three specific aims:

- to investigate awareness of the rights and duties of landlords, managing agents and tenants under the 1987 Act;

- to determine levels of satisfaction with the provisions of the legislation;

- to explore the conditions under which the provisions of the Act have been considered, used, or would be used in the future.

The research was designed to explore the practical experiences and any difficulties encountered by individuals who have made use of, or considered using the provisions of the Act. This is set in the general context of tenants housing experiences and their awareness and understanding of the ways in which their rights have been affected by the Act. In order to examine the potential impact of the provisions of the Act it was crucial to identify and explore any attitudinal or operational barriers to using the Act. From the point of view of managing agents and landlords it was essential to explore their understanding of their duties under the Act, as well as the effect that compliance had had on their managerial practices and in the resolution of day to day management problems.

1.4 Design and conduct of the study
Design and composition of the sample

The research employed a two stage design. The first stage was concerned with awareness and understanding of the Act's provisions amongst tenants, managing agents and landlords. In the second stage, experiences of using, or considered use of the Act were explored with tenants, managing agents and landlords. Reasons for not using legislation were also discussed. In addition, views about the practical application of the Act's provisions were sought from advisors (e.g. housing advice members) and advocates, such as legal advisors and solicitors.

The study was carried out using a combination of group discussions and in-depth investigatory interviews. These were held with tenants and leaseholders of flats, landlords and their agents, housing advisors, solicitors and professional bodies representing the interests of both landlords and tenants. Such methods were used because of the potential that they offer for exploring and examining awareness, attitudes and behaviour, in depth. It was also felt that given the range of housing circumstances and problems likely to be raised that a flexible and interactive approach to questioning would be the most appropriate.

The sample was purposively selected and designed to cover a range of different types of respondents, properties and geographical locations.

Four locations in England were selected providing wide geographical coverage and a range of different types of properties including mansion blocks, conversions and purpose-built blocks of flats. The four study areas selected were Brighton, Manchester, Paddington and Croydon. For a detailed discussion of how the study areas were selected see Appendix B. As the second stage of the study was concerned with people's experiences of using the Act the sample was restricted to those study areas (Paddington and Brighton) where greatest use of the Act had taken place.

In total 95 tenants, 10 managing agents, 10 landlords, and 16 advisors/advocates took part in the study.

Further details of the research design and methods of contacting respondents may be found in Appendix B.

The interviews

Stage one of the study, concerned with awareness and understanding of the Landlord and Tenant Act 1987, was carried out primarily through the use of 10 group discussions with tenants, as well as 12 interviews with managing agents (6) and landlords (6). The group discussions were carried out in local venues, the in-depth investigatory interviews at the respondent's place of work. In Stage two, people's experiences of the 1987 Act were explored through the use of in-depth investigatory interviews. In most cases, the discussions and interviews lasted around 1 hour.

All of the interviews and discussions were tape recorded, with the respondent's permission, and transcribed verbatim for subsequent analysis. The discussions and interviews used topic guides and exploratory interview techniques to explore awareness and understanding of the 1987 Act's provisions and to examine the impact of the new legislation on landlord-tenant relations and managerial practices. The majority of topic areas were covered with everyone but with flexible questioning to cope with widely differing housing circumstances and to allow issues of most relevance to the respondents to be pursued. Five topic guides were used to cover the range of respondents interviewed across the two stages of research study. Copies of these may be found in Appendix D.

Where respondents were not initially aware of the provisions of the 1987 Act, the interviewers described the main features to them. Concept display boards were used to enhance the interviewers explanation of the Act's provision - these are shown in Appendix E.

In a small number of instances (4) the opportunity arose to interview both parties (tenant and managing agent) to a dispute. Confidentiality was paramount and in such instances great care was taken to avoid identifying individuals or discussing individual disputes; the issues arising from such disputes were, however, discussed in detail.

The interviews were carried out between August 1990 and January 1991.

Analysis

Analysis was carried out from verbatim transcriptions of the tape recorded interviews and undertaken in two main stages. First, the transcribed material was charted in summary form within major subject areas. Second, the summarised and charted material was studied and categorised to examine people's understanding of the legislation, identify the circumstances in which it had been used, and any difficulties encountered in its application. The report was written from the charted material, with reference where appropriate, to the original interviews.

The report

The report is divided into six main sections. Chapter 2 provides a profile of the people interviewed and the type of properties represented with a particular focus on the types of housing problems they experience. The range of leasehold management structures encountered are also described. Chapter 3 considers the respondents' awareness of their rights and duties under the provisions of the Landlord and Tenant Act 1987. Chapter 4 explores respondents' experiences of the Act, taking each major provision in turn. Respondents were at varying stages of using the Act; in some cases legal action had been taken and was complete, in other cases respondents were still considering whether to exercise their rights. The chapter examines the impact of the Landlord and Tenant Act 1987 in addressing relevant landlord-tenant problems. Chapter 5 reviews the procedural aspects of the legislation, identifying a number of 'grey areas' and potential 'loopholes'. The chapter also examines a number of 'sharp' practices that managing agents and landlords were said to use as a way of circumventing the law. The final chapter addresses a number of practical issues that were raised in the context of the Landlord and Tenant Act 1987 but have relevance to housing legislation in general.

The qualitative nature of the information contained in this report cannot provide any statistical evidence of perceptions, attitudes or behaviours. The study's purpose is to explore people's understanding of the new legislation, the range of situations in which it has been used and the efficacy with which people felt the 1987 Act addressed their housing problems. The evidence presented in this report should be considered in this context and not as providing any numerical representation of the use or impact of the Landlord and Tenant Act 1987.

Chapter 2   A Profile of the Study Participants

The housing circumstances of the tenants interviewed varied considerably in terms of the type of property they lived in, the length of their tenure, and the nature of the housing difficulties (if any) they had experienced. Similarly, managing agents and landlords were selected to represent a broad range of property portfolios and types of management operation. By way of introduction a brief picture of the composition of the sample is given.

2.1 Sample profile

Across the two stages of the study 95 tenants, 10 landlords, 10 managing agents and 16 advisors were interviewed. Information was collected either through group discussions (Stage 1 tenants) or by individual depth interview (the remainder of the respondents). The breakdown of the sample by design stage and geographical location is shown in Table 2.1.

Table 2.1   **Sample composition**

	Tenants	Landlords	Managing agents	Advisors/ advocates
Stage 1				
Brighton	13	2	2	-
Croydon	21	2	1	-
Paddington	25	1	3	-
Manchester	14	1	-	-
Total	**73**	**6**	**6**	-
Stage 2				
Brighton	5			
Croydon	2	4[1]	4[2]	16
Paddington	13			
Manchester	2			
Total	**22**	**4**	**4**	**16**
Grand total	**95**	**10**	**10**	**16**[3]

[1]   All of the landlords interviewed were based in the London area, but had interests in other parts of the country, including Brighton and Manchester.

[2]   All of the managing agents interviewed were based in the London area; two managed properties in Brighton, one in Manchester. One managing agent had interests in a subsidiary company that owned a number of freeholds.

[3]   Includes 2 professional bodies representing tenants, 3 professional bodies representing the interests of landlords/managing agents, 5 housing advisors (local authority or independent) and 6 solicitors.

Tenants

In stage one of the study (awareness), tenants were selected to provide a broad spread of properties, types of tenure, and lengths of tenancy. Because of the small number of people who had used the 1987 legislation it was not possible to select respondents for stage two of the study according to the type of property in which they lived. In general, the criteria for inclusion in this stage was that tenants had made use of, or had considered using the legislation. Where possible, respondents with experience of at least one of the major provisions of the Act were included. The profile of tenants taking part in the study is shown in Table 2.2.

Managing agents and landlords

A wide range of managing agents and landlords took part in the study, in terms of their managerial and property portfolios. For example, in terms of rents, properties ranged from £100 to £1,200 per week; management and property portfolios ranged from 25 units to 10,000 units. Most of the managing agents specialised in residential property management, although the majority also had some interest in commercial properties. However, in most cases, it was residential management that formed the bulk of their management portfolio.

Most of their operations were purely managerial, although some stated that they held interests in both residential and commercial properties, usually through an associated or subsidiary company. In other cases it was less clear: a small number of managing agents while maintaining that their sole business concerned property management, were known through other sources, to hold property portfolios, usually through subsidiary companies. Most of the managing agents were either chartered surveyors or estate agents by profession. A range of different types of landlord were interviewed in the study. Most held the freeholds to properties as a form of capital investment from which they could also gain income through ground rents. Some, however, were either builders or property developers, whose primary wish was to sell on the freeholds once the building work was completed.

Advisors and advocates

Three different types of advisors were interviewed: solicitors, housing advice workers, and professional bodies representing the interests of either tenants, managing agents or landlords.

The solicitors (6) taking part in the study were all working in private practice although some provided a service to Citizen's Advice Bureaux, through which they were interviewed. Two solicitors also provided submissions to the study under the auspices of the Law Society. Five housing advisors were interviewed. They worked either through the local authority or independent advice agencies. The remaining advisors (5) were professional associations representing either the interests of tenants, managing agents, or landlords. The following organisations took part in the study: Federation of Private Residents Associations, Camden Federation of Private Tenants, Association of Residential Managing Agents, Small Landlords Association, and the British Property Federation.

2.2 Management structures
Purpose built blocks of flats

The majority of properties were managed either by the landlord or a managing agent. However, in other instances, a range of managerial arrangements were to be found. Management arrangements tended to be related to different types of property. For example, a scenario that commonly emerged in newer purpose-built blocks of flats was as follows. Landlords would grant a 'head lease' to a management company owned by the leaseholders. This company would then grant sub-leases on each of the flats in the building. It was common for each of the leaseholders to buy a share in the management company at the time of purchasing the flat. This was usually for the nominal amount of £1, although in one instance each share cost the leaseholders £100. When the leaseholder sold their flat, their share in the management company was also sold. In some cases the residents association and the management company were one and the same; in others their functions were separated. Management of the block was by the residents, in all cases through an elected committee. Ground rent was usually collected by the management company on behalf of the landlord, although in some cases ground rents were paid direct to the landlord by each individual leaseholder. In general, the landlord had little contact with the leaseholders. It is interesting to note, however, that despite the distant relationship most residents had with the landlord, many residents engaging in this style of management arrangement were mindful of adhering to the terms of their lease for fear of possible forfeiture.

Those respondents who rented their flat in a purpose built block were not included in these arrangements; they did not own a share in the management company, neither did they pay a separate service charge. In most cases they dealt directly with the landlord.

Table 2.2 **Profile of tenants**

	Stage 1	Stage 2	Total
Total	73	22	95
Tenure			
Rent	27	-	27
Lease	46	22	68
Property			
Conversion	36	11	47
Mansion block	13	7	20
New purpose built	24	4	28
No. of flats in building			
2 - 5	29	4	33
6 - 10	7	4	11
11 - 20	9	7	16
21 - 50	13	-	13
50 - 100	11	2	13
100+	3	3	6
Information not available	1	2	3
Length of tenancy			
Less than 1 year	7	1	8
1 - 3 years	24	2	26
3 - 10 years	16	12	28
10+ years	20	2	22
Information not available	6	5	11
Management			
Landlords	19	-	19
Managing agents	24	15	39
Residents Management Company	18[1]	5[2]	23
Information not available	12	2	14

[1] Management contracted out to Managing agents in 4 cases

[2] Management contracted out to Managing agents in 2 cases

Mansion blocks and conversions
Ownership of the freehold

Mansion blocks and properties that had been converted into flats tended to have a different set of managerial arrangements. Where the freehold had been purchased by the residents then a number of different arrangements were likely to occur. In most cases the freehold of the property was held by a company owned and run by the residents; they also held a share in this company, usually of a nominal value. In one mansion block, however, there were only two shares in the 'freehold' company, one held by the residents' solicitors, the other by the accountants to the resident-owned management company. The company holding the freehold then offered a lease to each of the residents.

In some of the properties not all of the residents bought a lease, preferring to continue to rent their accommodation. In one mansion block where this amounted to a substantial number of the flats (50 out of 167), the leases to the rented flats were bought by an investment company approved by the remainder of the residents. The investment company held 50 shares in the company that owned the freehold.

A converted house in Brighton had an alternative arrangement. Consisting of 19 flats, one of which was rented, the resident-owned company holding the freehold to the property also owned the lease to this flat. A condition of the mortgage lender meant that when the flat was sold, none of the existing leaseholders should benefit from any increase in the value of the flat. All profits were to be returned to the company owing the freehold and used to maintain the property as a whole.

In one property, a Brighton conversion, the residents continued to pay a ground rent, but rather than being paid to an 'external' landlord, it was paid to their own company that held the freehold. The residents had yet to decide exactly how to use this money, but thought that it might form the basis of a property maintenance 'sinking fund'. In the same property, while all of those who had purchased a lease when the freehold was sold to the resident-owned company, their nominal share in this company was not necessarily sold when they sold their flat. Because some of the original purchasers had sold their flats, this block was now in the position where the company owning the freehold was only partly owned by the current leaseholders. To date they had not experienced any difficulties but had begun to wonder whether such an arrangement could be problematic in the future.

Where the freehold was not owned by the residents, then the property was managed either by the landlord or a managing agent on their behalf. In one Paddington mansion block, for example, a head lease had been granted to the residents association, which in turn granted a number of sub-leases. The rented flats in the block were owned by an investment company. The freehold was owned by an off-shore company based in Liberia, which in turn was owned by a trust based in Jersey. The residents did not have the power to manage the building; the appointment of the managing agent was determined by the freeholder.

Types of Management

In most cases where the residents had formed a management company this was a subsidiary of the company that owned the freehold. In one mansion block, however, the position was reversed, primarily because the company owning the freehold had *"very little capital turnover"*. Where the number of flats was small (generally under 20) the residents usually carried out the management of the building. Decisions were primarily made through the residents' association. In the two instances where there were a substantial number of flats (140 and 167, both mansion blocks in Paddington) the management task had been contracted out. In both cases, the management and accountancy functions had been kept apart by appointing separate managing agents and accountants.

Views about the nature of property management were highly polarised. Many respondents had not experienced difficulties in ensuring that the property was adequately maintained; they were often very happy with the management provided by the landlord or their agent. People living in newer-purpose built properties were less likely to raise problems of a management related nature. Respondents living in mansion blocks and conversions tended to raise the most concerns about the maintenance of the building. Where people had experienced difficulties, they tended to favour other forms of management in which neither the landlord or managing agent were involved.

People perceived both advantages and disadvantages with either self or 'external' management. The chief objections to management by a landlord or managing agent were a general lack of control, for example, the timing of work carried out, the standard of building works; the possibility of high service charges; lack of accountability; and the potential for high management charges. Many conceded, however, that where management was properly carried out by landlords or their agents tenants benefited by being able to pass the responsibility (other than financial) for the upkeep of the building to another party. By contrast, those who managed the building themselves (including those who employed managing agents) said that there were considerable advantages: total control over the maintenance of the building and the financial accounting, and either no, or reduced, management charges. The disadvantages, however, were that it was a *"highly responsible position", requiring considerable amounts of time, effort and expertise. Additional disadvantages included the difficulty of involving 'reluctant volunteers' to help with the management task, collecting service charge arrears, financial accounting,* and that there was *"no guarantee what everyone will be happy"*. However, these disadvantages were felt to be considerably outweighed by the advantages.

It is interesting that a number of landlords also favoured self-management by residents. In part, this was because it meant that they had no responsibility for the building. However, some also felt that it provided an excellent way of reducing tensions between the landlord and the tenant. A number of managing agents were also in favour of the control of property maintenance being passed to the tenants. They, too, argued that it would reduce the levels of disputes about management as they would no longer be seen as *"an agent of the landlord"*. In addition, they thought it might also force the *"cowboy agents"* out of the market which would have a beneficial effect on the industry as a whole.

> *"It seems to me that there are a lot of cowboys in the field, just there to make a fast buck ... and many of them are in with the landlord ... they are there just to cream as much money as they can ... I have had situations where the landlord has asked me to do something I didn't think was right ... I managed to resolve that one, but it does put us in a difficult situation ... like a go-between. Many of my landlords are very business like and I like to think that we are well respected, but I know some [agents] who aren't ... I would be quite happy to manage on behalf of tenants ... I think it would be better in the long run as we would have a relationship with just one party ... I think that is the way it will go in the future ... the property market is so bad now that many landlords are lucky if they get a decent return ... 4% return was what one of my clients reckoned he was getting on his residential portfolio. Commercial is quite different, but no, I'd be very happy to act on behalf of tenants."* (Paddington, Managing agent. Manages approximately 90 blocks, the largest with 250 units, mainly in the Greater London area.)

2.3 Housing problems

A wide range of problems emerged in our discussions with people who leased or rented their accommodation. These problems generally fell into one of three categories: problems with the provision of services; communication with the landlord and/or managing agent; and issues arising from a mismatch between people's expectations and the services with which they are provided. Many of the problems to arise are of direct relevance to any discussion of the Landlord and Tenant Act 1987, others are of a more general nature. In particular, it was tenants who rented their accommodation who raised problems that fell outside the ambit of the 1987 Act. We provide here an overview of the housing problems experienced by tenants taking part in the study. These will be discussed more fully in relation to the 1987 Act in Chapters 3 and 4.

Problems with the provision of services

The majority of complaints centred on the provision of services, repairs, maintenance and accounting. These are detailed in summary form in Table 2.3. People who rented their accommodation ('renters') tended to raise different housing issues to those who leased their accommodation. Leaseholders were generally concerned with the fabric of the building, including issues such as the building's security, entryphones, and the condition of the common parts. While renters shared some of these concerns their security of tenure and experiences of landlords gaining access to their flats without permission were said to be of greater significance to them.

Communication with the landlord/managing agent

It was very apparent, talking to all parties that some managing agents and landlords kept tenants at a distance and consulted with them as little as possible. In a small number of cases, 'consultation' only occurred through solicitors. One landlord was reported as saying that he would willingly talk to the tenants in person, but only in the presence of his solicitor, for which the tenants would have to pay.

Others, however, adopted quite a different approach. They felt that a 'trouble shooting' approach was the best; it kept both the tenants and managing agents informed and ensured that any problems that arose were dealt with before they become major issues. Each agent had their own strategy. By ways of example, one managing agent said that he talked to a representative of the block of flats, either a tenant or the residents association on a weekly basis to ascertain whether there are any problems. It is a fairly recent innovation - prior to this the company had a strategy by which tenants would ring in with problems which could then be sorted out through discussion with the landlord. Problems are now 'headed off' before they escalate. Although he said that this might appear to be a a time consuming method of managing property, it was his view that it was a beneficial strategy: it saved enormous amounts of time and had a very beneficial effect on the relationship between tenants, managing agents and landlords.

Many people talked about the poor communication they had with their landlord or managing agent. In discussing the communication between tenants and landlords it is important to distinguish between that which is legally required (e.g. the provision of a landlord's name and address, service charge demands, and end of year accounts) and that which is undertaken in addition to the minimum required by statute. Three types of communication problem emerged: making contact with the landlord, obtaining and understanding documents provided by the landlord or managing agent, and the resolution of problems.

Most respondents were aware of their landlord's name and address. This was true for all of those who rented their accommodation; many met their landlord or the agent on a regular basis when the rent was due. However, some leaseholders had experienced difficulties in obtaining a contact address. For example, the landlord's address had never been provided; managing agents refusal to divulge the landlord's address; a false name and/or address was given, either by the landlord or their agent.

In other instances a name and address were available but this was sometimes an accommodation address, or else letters and phone calls remained unanswered. Respondents often said that where they were able to make contact, action was sometimes only taken after a considerable number of requests, either verbal or written; many had to resort to the threat of legal action before the landlord responded.

Landlords and managing agents were often said to change without any notification. Sometimes, respondents found that the landlord had changed managing agents in response to their threat of court action; often it took many months before the identity of the new managing agent become clear. In other instances, the name of the agent changed but the address remained the same. Similarly, many respondents were confident that there had been a change of freeholder, often said to be demonstrated by a change in management style, but the identity of the new freeholder remained hidden.

Landlords and managing agents are required by statute to provide details of the service charge and end of year account. In many cases this was complied with and respondents were happy with the information, and simply paid the service charge demand because *"it seemed reasonable"*. Others, however, had considerable difficulty in obtaining service charge accounts; others found that they contained major discrepancies, such as items charged for but not supplied or not functioning, or errors of addition in the accounts, in some cases amounting to hundreds, or even thousands, of pounds. Many people commented that the accounts were supplied in a form that were not understandable to the lay person, for example, in the form of company accounts.

The need for simple, yet clear, fully itemised accounts emerged as a key requirement by tenants, many feeling that it was their right to receive simple, itemised accounts within the existing management fee. Many of the managing agents were happy to comply with this. However, they commented that, first, in their experience tenants did not want detailed accounts. Second, if they could find a more user-friendly way of presenting accounts they would do so, but tenants would have to be aware of the cost implications. Some managing agents were not keen to go to additional lengths in producing such information: *"It's none of their business"* said one managing agent, *"We're managing properties, we're not accountants"*, said another.

Mismatches between expectations and the services provided

It was a commonly held view by managing agents and landlords that some tenants expected far more services than were stipulated in the lease or paid for in the service charge. This was felt to occur for two main reasons: first, tenants were not familiar with the terms of their lease, and second, they had unrealistic expectations of landlords and managing agents.

Overwhelmingly, from all concerned there was a view that few leaseholders read and understood the content of the lease they had signed when they bought their flat. In part this was thought to be because of their readability of leases (an issue discussed in Chapter 6), but also because people see the signing of leases as a formality and something *"They have to do if they want the flat, they don't have any option"*. It was mentioned many times that some leaseholders did not really understand the concept of a lease, neither did they fully appreciate the nature of service charges or demands for maintenance.

One managing agent described an incident that is of particular relevance to this point. Under the terms of the lease, tenants in one of the blocks he managed made payments to a long term maintenance fund. Under the lease the block was redecorated every four years. A number of tenants were said to become very hostile because they felt they were paying for services that were not being carried out. Yet, as the agent pointed out, the monies were accruing in readiness for the next time the building was to be painted. In this instance, the leaseholders had neither understood the contract that they had entered into when they bought their flat, nor the nature of owning leasehold property.

It also emerged that by virtue of paying a service charge, some leaseholders felt that they were entitled to call upon the services of the managing agent and landlord at any time. This, too, was apparent from discussions with all parties concerned. For example, a Brighton landlord described a leaseholder who rang him in the early hours of the morning to repair the hot water system in her flat. Similarly, a managing agent mentioned a leaseholder who *"continually pestered me"* to replace her cracked wash hand basin, even though it was not the responsibility of the landlord or managing agent to do so.

Problems arising out of these differing expectations were very common. As one managing agent argued, it was not in anyone's interest for this to occur. He conceded that in many instances, leaseholders were justified in their complaints about the services provided - *"there's a lot of cowboys and rip-off merchants out there"*. Equally, many complaints were not felt to be justified and thought to result from a leaseholder's incorrect expectations of the duties of a managing agent or landlord. We continue this discussion and put forward a number of suggested solutions to these problems in Chapter 6.

Table 2.3 **Difficulties experienced with the provision of repairs and services**

Leaseholders

Repairs	- not carried out, even when promised - lengthy delays (2 years mentioned) - poor quality repairs, often having to be re-done, usually at additional expense to service charge payers - inadequate supervision and inspection
Refurbishment	- too little remedial work carried out - too much work carried out; providing unnecessary facilities such as marble lined entrance ways - maintenance carried out when not necessary, but simply to fulfil terms of the leaes
Costs	- costs unrealistically high - cost overruns - service charges increasing at a rate faster than the cost of services provided - quotes 'rigged' by landlords/managing agents - refusal to acknowledge leaseholders estimates - the same company always employed to do works - an association with the landlord/managing agent suspected
Consultation	- refusal to consult over estimates and/or need for works - tenants' observations ignored
Services	- services required under the terms of the lease, such as cleaning, gardening, etc not provided - services provided at lower level/frequency than required - services charged for but either not provided or not functioning (e.g. entryphone)
Accounting	- difficulty in obtaining accounts - complicated or *"indecipherable"* accounts - insufficient itemisation of accounts - accounts that do not add up (£5,000 adrift in one case) - charges made that are higher than 'cost' (e.g. 10% charged on all bills, **in addition to** the management charge) - services charged for but not provided
Insurance	- landlord reluctant/refused to provide details - management charge added to insurance premium - landlord's commission not declared or passed to the service charge account - buildings under insured or not insured - tenants requests to change management company ignored - landlord pockets money from insurance claims

Renters

Repairs	- not carried out - poor quality - delays
Security	- landlords gain access to tenants' flats without permission
Costs	- rents perceived as *"unfairly high"* for the condition of the building

Chapter 3   Awareness and Understanding of the Landlord and Tenant Act 1987

This chapter explores respondents' awareness of the provisions of the Landlord and Tenant Act 1987. It sets the scene for the next chapter, in which respondents' views about the Act and their experiences of using it are considered. The analysis presented in this chapter is primarily based on the interviews and discussions with respondents taking part in stage one of the study (73 tenants, 6 managing agents and 6 landlords); where relevant, however, views about the legislation expressed by the stage two respondents are included.

The chapter begins by looking at respondents' general awareness of the Act and then explores their views about the new legislation. However, as the majority of the respondents had little or no experience of using the Act, their comments are confined to the 'principle' of the Act, rather than their practical application.

3.1 General awareness of the Landlord and Tenant Act 1987
General awareness
Tenants

Among tenants, awareness of the Act, either by name or by principle, was relatively low. Only a small proportion of respondents had heard of the Act whilst very few had any detailed knowledge or understanding of the Act's provisions.

There were a few exceptions to this. For example, one man said that he had read the Act; another recognised the overall principle of the new legislation:

> *"I understand that it was an Act trying to balance up the rights and wrongs, with landlords still retaining their rights and tenants retaining theirs - it had to be more even-handed"* (Brighton Leaseholder, purpose-built block of flats.)

Others recalled individual features of the Act. For example, a handful of people had either heard of the right of first refusal or recalled that they were entitled to be consulted about building works.

In some instances people remembered the spirit of the legislation but had misunderstood how it worked in practice. For example, one respondent, living in a newer purpose-built block of flats in the Paddington study area, said that she had heard through the residents' association that they were entitled to appoint a managing agent, but, incorrectly, she thought this was without reference to the freeholder.

Of the 73 people who attended one of the ten group discussions, 17 were living in accommodation where the building was managed by the residents themselves. Overall, this represented nine independently run management companies. In a quarter of cases respondents were either directors of the company or held positions, usually the chair, on the company's management committee. Very few of these respondents were aware of the 1987 Act. Of the four who spontaneously recognised the new legislation none were aware of all of the Act's major provisions; knowledge of the more detailed and procedural aspects of the legislation was very patchy.

None of these respondents were aware that their 'independent' management companies had the same duties under the 1987 Act as landlords or their managing agents.

Managing agents

All of the managing agents were aware of the 1987 Act; one was very familiar with the Act and had been involved in making submissions to the Nugee Committee of Inquiry. Since it had passed onto the statute books he had regularly given lectures about it and its implications for residential management. The remainder were all familiar with the main provisions of the Act although most confessed to having varying degrees of familiarity with the 'fine detail'. In general, the managing agents were most familiar with three provisions of the Act - the right of first refusal (Part I), the calculation and accounting of service charges (Part V - Sections 41 and 42), and the information to be provided about the landlord (Part VI) - these were the provisions with which they dealt most frequently. In general, they were not concerned at their lack of familiarity with the procedural details of the Act. They felt that it was not possible to be fully conversant with all the housing legislation whilst also providing a management service. Where problems arose they had recourse either to their solicitors, in-house legal advisors, specialist technical manuals or their professional bodies (particularly the Royal Institute of Chartered Surveyors) for professional advice.

Landlords

Landlords, by contrast, were less familiar with the 1987 Act, often confusing it with the Housing Act 1988. Of the six landlords interviewed in the first stage, one was well versed in the provisions of the Act and many of the procedures involved. Another could not recall the Act or any of its features. The remainder had heard of the Act but their knowledge of the Act's provisions was sketchy and restricted only to the major features.

Misconceptions

It was apparent that tenants were very confused about their rights and had little understanding of the housing legislation and how it applied to them. We pointed to a difference between leaseholders and renters in Chapter 2 concerning the housing issues they raised during the group discussions. There was also a difference in their awareness of housing legislation. Those who rented their accommodation were more likely to discuss their rights, particularly where they had experience of the 'assured shorthold tenancies' introduced in the Housing Act 1988. In discussing 'rights', most renters referred to the Housing Act 1988; few recognised the 1987 legislation. Where people had bought a lease, overall, they were less likely to be aware of their housing rights.

Very often there was considerable confusion about the various pieces of legislation that had been introduced. Many confused the Landlord and Tenant Act 1987 with other pieces of housing legislation. A small number referred to the Landlord and Tenant Act 1985 and were not aware of their new rights under the 1987 Act. More frequently, however, respondents thought that the 1987 Act was to do with *"fair rents"*, *"market rents"*, and the *"erosion of security of tenure"*, confusing these with the provisions of the Housing Act 1988. The greatest confusion between these two Acts appeared to occur in those areas where there had been extensive publicity about the Housing Act 1988.

Assimilating new legislation

As we have seen, general levels of awareness about the 1987 Act were low amongst tenants, and rather patchy amongst landlords.

The fact that tenants' awareness of the Act, either by name or by principle, was low is not surprising. There are two issues that are of importance. First, a number of studies concerned with the impact of new legislation have indicated that the recall or recognition of new rights or duties is often low because people tend to operate on a 'need to know' basis. It is only when a problem arises that the majority of people ascertain their rights and seek out methods of redress. Second, studies have also shown that, in general, people do not assimilate and recall information in terms of an Act or a piece of legislation. Rather, they recall isolated, but relevant (to them) pieces of information, often without any attributable source.

In practice, this therefore means that many tenants are not aware of their rights (or duties) under new legislation. This can be particularly problematic where there is a need to take action within strict time limits, as in the Landlord and Tenant Act 1987.

While managing agents also operated, to some extent, on a 'need to know' basis, it was clear that their understanding and appreciation of the provisions of the 1987 Act were of a different magnitude. Although the fine detail of the Act was not necessarily at their fingertips they all felt that they could access the relevant information with little difficulty.

As we have seen, landlords were generally sketchy in their understanding of the 1987 Act. In some instances they were contravening the provisions of the Act because of their lack of familiarity with the new legislation.

It is very apparent that there is a need for a system to distribute and disseminate the key features of newly introduced legislation. Amongst tenants, in particular, there was a considerable body of opinion in favour of better publicity for new legislation. We return to a detailed discussion of this issue in Chapter 6.

3.2 General views about the Landlord and Tenant Act 1987

In this section we review respondents' general views about the 1987 Act drawing on the opinions of all the respondents taking part in both stages of the study. Because awareness of the legislation was so low amongst the stage one tenants it was necessary to stimulate discussion about the 1987 Act using concept boards containing the main features of the Act - Appendix E. (Throughout this report we discuss the Act's provisions in relation to the topics encompassed by these concept boards.) As few people attending the group discussions had any experience of using the Act, their opinions are, necessarily, confined to the 'principle' of the legislation. This is supplemented by the experiences of those people taking part in the second stage of the study. We confine ourselves in this section to general views about the relevance and potential usefulness of the Act. Respondents' experiences of using the legislation and a discussion of its efficacy will be presented in Chapters 4 and 5.

Tenants

Overall, tenants welcomed the new legislation and found that the Act provided rights that they felt would be useful to them. However, opinions about the Act were strongly divided between those who had purchased a lease (leaseholders) and those who paid rent (renters) for their accommodation. In each case, their generally favourable opinion of the new legislation was tempered by a number of conditions.

Leaseholders were the most enthusiastic about the Act and, in general, felt that it had the potential to redress the balance between the landlord and themselves. However, there were four major features which were felt to seriously impair the overall usefulness of the Act. First, many felt that while some of the provisions were potentially very useful in regulating the day to day managerial affairs between the landlord and the leaseholder (e.g. the provisions concerned with service charges, building insurance, and the right to certain information about the landlord) there was a general feeling that enforcement could be problematic if the landlord or managing agent were determined not to comply. The Act was often described as *"toothless"* and in this context meant that where landlords failed to comply there was little in the way of penalties or sanctions. For example, the withholding of service charge monies for non-compliance under Section 47 of the Act (landlord's name and address to appear on all written documents) was not thought to be particularly significant. Landlords were thought to be unlikely to feel penalised by this; it was the fabric of the building and the people living in it who were thought to suffer most because maintenance would cease to be carried out. Most tenants felt that there should be a financial penalty for non-compliance with this and all other parts of the Act. That way, they argued, if non-compliance meant that landlords would suffer financially, there was a greater likelihood that they would meet their obligations under the Act.

Second, the Act makes provisions in many instances for the resolution of difficulties or disputes to be addressed in court. Similarly, non-compliance may also be resolved by court action. Overwhelmingly, tenants felt that for many issues (including service charges) court action was likely to cost more than the problem they were trying to resolve. There was a general feeling that going to court was not the most appropriate solution; it would be burdensome in terms of the time taken to resolve a problem and the likely cost entailed. This was a very significant issue raised many times and in a variety of different circumstances. We return to a detailed discussion of this point in Chapter 6.

Issues concerning the right of first refusal form the third problem area identified by tenants. First, some felt that this provision did not go far enough and should be an automatic 'right to buy'. Others, however, felt that this was not acceptable as it amounted to the compulsory purchase of another person's property. Second, the requirement for the purchase to be collective was very often thought to be a hinderance. In this context, a number of tenants thought that the right of first refusal should be amended so that a person would be able to purchase their flat on an individual basis, rather than collectively.

Fourth, bearing in mind the perceived limitations of the Act discussed so far, and related primarily to Parts I (Right of first refusal), V (Management) and VI (Information) of the Act, most tenants felt that the remainder of the legislation was only likely to be used 'in extremis'. Consequently they felt that Parts II (Appointment of managers), III (Compulsory acquisition) and IV (Variation of leases) of the Act were of little relevance to them in solving their housing problems.

Those who rented their accommodation were less enthusiastic about the 1987 Act, finding little in the legislation that was of interest or use to them. There were four issues in particular that reduced the relevance of the 1987 Act. First, Section VI (Information to be provided to tenants) only applies where a separate and variable service charge is paid. None of the renters in this study conformed to this requirement and were, therefore, excluded from this part of the Act. It is noteworthy that amongst all the respondents in the study (including landlords, managing agents and advisors) none had any experience or knowledge of people who paid a service charge in addition to their rent. Many felt that this unfairly discriminated against people who paid rent for their accommodation: there was a sizeable body of opinion that these provisions should be extended to cover renters who do not pay a separate and variable service charge. Second, while the right of first refusal was potentially attractive in principle there was a general view amongst renters that because they were likely to be at the lower end of the earnings scale, the right was of little practical use to them. Third, particularly for younger people who tended to be short-term tenants, the legislation was felt to be too cumbersome and incorporate lengthy consultation periods (perceived as delays) which were inappropriate for their type of tenancy. Fourth, many people who rented were unwilling to use the legislation or take court action under the 1987 Act for fear of reprisal from their landlord or managing agent. Many felt that it was not worth pursuing their rights or taking action (either court action or withholding payments) under the Landlord and Tenant Act 1987 because of the perceived likelihood of *"hassle"* and *"harassment"* from their landlords or agents.

Managing agents and landlords

Overall, managing agents felt that the majority of provisions in the 1987 Act were *"correct and proper"*. Many said that some provisions, notably those concerning information about the landlord, buildings insurance, the calculation of service charges, and the holding of service charge money in trust were simply a reflection of good management practices which they already operated. Some were concerned at the increased amount of paperwork that the Act was said to generate, others were concerned at the increase in accounting that had occurred as a result of Section 42 (holding service charge contribution in trust). In many cases, however, this increase in cost had been defrayed by increasing their management fees.

There was universal praise for Part IV (variation of leases) although some felt the procedures to be cumbersome. Similarly, most felt that Parts I (Right of first refusal), II (Appointment of managers) and III (Compulsory acquisition) were *"good pieces of legislation"*, in principle, although there was some feeling that the appointment of a manager and compulsory acquisition (Parts II and III, respectively) were likely to be rarely used and only in extreme circumstances. This was because of the time and expense of litigation thought likely to be incurred in using these provisions. A small number of managing agents felt that compulsory acquisition (Part III) was unnecessary. This was for two reasons. First, they held a fundamental objection to the right of any person being able to compulsorily acquire another person's property. Second, they felt that suitable means of redress were already provided under Part II of the Act (Appointment of managers by the court).

The right of first refusal was generally felt to be acceptable - some simply thought it was courteous to offer the building to their existing tenants. A small number, however, objected to this provision. *"The landlord should be able to sell to whoever they wish"*, it was argued, *"it is their property after all ... leaseholders have simply bought a timed interest in the freeholders' property"*. *Most of the managing agents felt that Part I was unnecessarily cumbersome, some considering that the time periods built into the legislation would have the effect of depressing the price that the landlord could obtain for the property"*.

Landlords were generally accepting of the new legislation, and in common with the managing agents interviewed felt that many of the provisions were a formality with which they already complied. Again, most felt that the rights conferred on tenants were acceptable and morally right; they felt though that the balance between landlord and tenant had been tipped unnecessarily in the tenant's favour. The right of first refusal was raised in this context. In particular, the time scale was felt to have a deleterious effect on the sale price of the property. Similarly, while landlords felt that it was fair to inform tenants of the process by which service charges are calculated, it was also felt that the Act did not go far enough and should have provided landlords with the means to re-coup unpaid service charge money quickly and efficiently.

A number of landlords commented how the 1987 legislation was *"just another burden"*. In the eyes of another landlord the Act *"had nuisance value, but we still do what we want ... we can get round it"*.

Advisors

Two types of advisor were interviewed, those broadly representing the tenant (e.g. local authority housing advice workers, and local 'housing project' workers) which we refer to here as 'tenants' advisors' and those who represented the interests of managing agents and landlords, which we refer to as 'commercial advisors'. While, overall, there was general agreement that the Act was beneficial, there were also sharp divisions in opinion about some of the Act's provisions. Parts IV (Variation of leases), V (Management) and VI (Information) of the Act generally met with praise; most advisors, however, felt that the procedures incorporated into Parts V and VI were unnecessarily bureaucratic. Advisors representing the landlords and managing agents felt that these provisions were administratively burdensome and expensive, although most said that the cost would be offset by increasing their management fees. Advisors representing tenants, by contrast, felt that in these areas the Act was potentially ineffectual for two reasons: the lack of any financial penalty for non-compliance with the Act's provisions and the need to go to court to resolve disputes over relatively small amounts of money.

Appointment of managers (Part II) by the court and compulsory acquisition (Part III) were generally welcomed by the 'tenants advisors' although the degree of expertise required and the likely costs involved in using these parts of the Act were often commented upon. The 'commercial advisors', however, felt that these provisions were unlikely to be used very often. Because these parts of the Act had been little used at the time of the study most preferred to *"reserve judgement"*. However, there were some objections, partly on the grounds of procedural complexity and partly because they felt, in the case of Part III (Compulsory acquisition), that it was morally unjustifiable to compulsorily acquire another person's property. These objections will be more fully discussed in the next chapter.

The right of first refusal was often very contentious. Tenants' advisors tended to be in agreement with those they represented; the right was very welcome but reservations were expressed about the procedures required by the Act; many felt that the right should be extended to become a 'right to buy'. By contrast, commercial advisors tended to adopt similar views to those of the managing agents and landlords; the legislation was overly bureaucratic; the time periods specified were felt to be too long; and the legislation would depress property prices.

3.3 Awareness and views about the individual provisions of the Landlord and Tenant Act 1987

In the following section we discuss each of the Act's main provisions in turn, looking at respondents' awareness of the provisions and their views about the legislation. We discuss eight main provisions that conform to the concept boards used in the group discussions and shown in Appendix E.

It is useful to note that while managing agents were generally aware of all of the 1987 Act's provisions, in varying degrees of detail, tenants, and to some extent landlords, tended only to be familiar with those provisions with which they had experience. Typically, Parts I (Right of first refusal), V (Management of leasehold properties), and VI (Information to be provided to tenants) fell into this category. Advisors, too, had a rather sketchy understanding of the Act. Those who tended to deal mainly with rented accommodation were least likely to be aware of all of the Act's provisions, while others were more likely to be familiar with those parts of the Act (typically Parts I, V, and VI) that covered regularly occurring problems.

Information about the landlord
Providing the landlord's name and address

Many of the tenants were aware that they were entitled to know the name and address of their landlord. A small number thought that this had always been the case and were not aware that the original entitlement to such information became a legal requirement under the Landlord and Tenant Act 1985. Opinion was divided over the usefulness of having the landlord's name and address; some felt that the information was not relevant to them although conceded that should there ever be a problem such information would be invaluable. By contrast, others, who had usually experienced some form of difficulty, thought that the landlord's name and address was essential.

Although the majority received invoices and demands for payment, such as for service charges, which included the landlord's name and address, a small number of respondents received bills which included only the managing agents' name and address. In general, this group of people, who were mostly living in purpose built blocks of flats, did not know the identity of their landlord. The majority of tenants were not aware that demands for payment must include the landlord's name and address.

It is interesting that one leaseholder talking on behalf of the residents of a self-managed block of flats (freehold owned by a builder, head lease purchased by resident-owned management company) said that they did not provide the landlord's name and address on any documents for three reasons: the management company 'owned' the lease and made all the decisions concerning the management of the building; the freeholder had no practical interest in the building, receiving only a token sum in ground rent; and *"residents haven't asked for this [information] and probably aren't interested anyway"*. This respondent was not aware that other residents in the block were legally entitled to such information.

All of the managing agents were aware of the legal duty to provide the landlord's name and address on demands for money and most complied with this. One, however, only provided the landlord's name saying that they had yet to seek their client's permission to divulge an address. They were keen to comply with the legislation and said that this deficiency would soon be corrected when new computer software for the generation of service charge demands had been installed.

Landlords were less aware of their duties under this provision of the Act although all but one of them complied with the law. This landlord had adopted the practice of including the charge for ground rent in the service charge and could see no reason why tenants should be given, or need, the landlord's name and address under any circumstances.

Withholding payment

None of the tenants were aware that they had a right to withhold payment of service charges where the landlord's name and address is not given. A small number had resorted to this tactic and *"crossed my fingers in the hope that nothing will go wrong"*. However, in all cases this was due to reasons of poor or inadequate services being provided and was not related to Section 47 of the Act. A handful of the tenants were aware of their right to search Land Registry records; one person 'assumed' that this would be the case. A small number of tenants had used the Land Register in an attempt to locate their landlord.

While all of the managing agents were aware that tenants had the right to withhold payment if the legal requirement to provide a contact address was breached, not all were aware of a tenants' right to search the Land Register. Few of the landlords spontaneously recalled the tenants' right to withhold payment or search the Land Register. With the exception of one landlord all the remaining managing agents and landlords felt that this was a right that would rarely need to be exercised, but nevertheless felt that the duty to provide a contact name and address was *"absolutely right"*.

Service charges and consultations over building works
Service charge accounting and consultation

The majority of tenants were aware that they were entitled to some form of account of the service charge monies paid, although only about half attributed this right to the Landlord and Tenant Act 1987. Far fewer were aware that they had a legal right to inspect receipts or to challenge the amount of money demanded; only a small number of respondents said that they had inspected service charge receipts.

The group discussions evidenced a wide range of ways in which managing agents and landlords informed tenants about service charges. At one extreme, some tenants received an annual demand for payment with no breakdown of how the service charge monies had been spent in the previous year. At the other extreme, one tenant received a quarterly demand together with a detailed breakdown of how the service charge had been spent in the previous quarter. The majority of people, however, received an annual statement of account giving various amounts of information about how the service charge monies had been used - these varied in detail and their perceived usefulness. It is interesting that those people who said that they had the clearest understanding of how the service charge money was spent tended to be the most aware of their rights under the Act, as well as having the fewest complaints about how the money had been spent.

All of the managing agents and most of the landlords produced service charge accounts. In some instances this was simply an annual balance sheet, in others it was presented in the form of a bank statement with notes attached. Not all of this group of respondents were aware that they had a legal duty under the 1987 Act to provide service charge accounts, although most did so because it was a requirement stipulated by the lease. Some said that although they could produce itemised statements, they did not do so. This was partly because they believed that tenants did not want any more information and partly because they said it would cost more to do so, which would have to be passed on to the tenants through the service charge.

Consultation about building works

Very few tenants were aware that they were entitled under the 1987 Act to be consulted about building works, to see estimates and to challenge the work or cost of the work. Of those who were aware, and in general, these were residents living in converted flats, only a handful mentioned a consultation threshold. They were all unaware of the new threshold introduced with the 1987 Act (£1,000 or £50 per dwelling) and mentioned thresholds of £500 or £25 per flat. Some assumed that they had this right but did not link it to any legislation.

Respondents representing resident owned management companies were also not aware of tenants' entitlement to be consulted about building works. Some of them did so but rarely provided detailed specifications.

All of the managing agents were aware of the requirement to consult tenants over building works although each had a different view of the consultation threshold. For one it was *"£1,000, £50 per dwelling, whichever is greater"* (as required by the 1987 Act). For others it was *"anything major"*, *"£25 per flat"*, or *"whenever necessary"*.

Of the six landlords interviewed in stage one of the study, only three were aware of the requirement to consult tenants over building works and only two of these were aware of a consultation threshold. One had stopped sending estimates to tenants as *"you get too many responses"*.

Holding service charge money in trust	Very few tenants were aware that service charge money should be held 'in trust'. Most assumed that this money went into the *"general coffers of the landlord"*; others were aware that the money was held by the managing agents, but again, thought it went into a general fund. Some, simply had no idea where the money went, while a few thought it 'common sense' that service charge money was held in a separate account.

Managing agents were very aware that service charge payments were held in trust under the Landlord and Tenant Act 1987. By contrast, few of the landlords interviewed knew about this provision.

Insurance of the property	Overall, tenants had little awareness of their right to know about the insurance cover for the property; less than a dozen said that they knew which insurance company was being used or had received details of the insurance cover - this was primarily those who were living in purpose-built blocks of flats. Very often, tenants had found out about the property insurance by accident, for example when making a claim or when first buying the property and the building society had demanded to see the insurance cover.

For the majority of tenants, however, 'building insurance' was simply an entry on their service charge account. Some had not thought about the type of insurance that covered the property, while a small number of others felt that they had sufficient information.

None of the tenants were aware that they had the right to challenge the landlords' choice of insurance company and policy; when told about the facility to reach agreement over the choice of insurance company by applying to the court for a variation of the lease, there was a general feeling that this was a cumbersome and expensive method of solving an essentially simple problem.

Only a handful of tenants knew that they could notify insurance companies direct of any claims. A couple had done this and been successful. In other instances, the landlord or managing agent had insisted that they dealt with any claims; in another instance the insurance company had refused to deal with the tenants' claim, referring it to the landlord for approval.

Four tenants who attended one of the group discussions, represented four different 'self-managed' blocks of flats. Although they all allowed easy access to the insurance documents, some holding copies that could be taken away for inspection, none of these were aware of the tenants' right to know about the property insurance under the Landlord and Tenant Act 1987. This was typical of the majority of people representing self-managed blocks of flats.

Managing agents and landlords were not universally aware of the provisions relating to property insurance. A small number automatically provided such information - one managing agent described an 'insurance pack' containing details of the insurer, amount insured and the policy coverage. The remainder would provide the information if requested, although none had been asked to do so. Most felt this was a useful, albeit rarely used, piece of legislation; only one landlord felt it 'burdensome' and expensive to comply with. Most were aware that tenants could notify the insurance company direct.

The role of tenants/residents associations

The role of tenants associations (TAs) tended to be a minor issue amongst the tenants attending the group discussions. In total, eight tenants in the stage one discussions were members, representing seven different associations. They ranged across a variety of different properties, and were spread across the four study areas. Members of tenants associations tended to be more aware of the rights of TAs than others, although their knowledge was often patchy.

Most of the managing agents, but few of the landlords, were aware of their general obligations towards tenants associations; one managing agent did not know he had to provide a detailed specification of building work to the TA. Those who were not aware of the provisions covering TAs, on the whole, did not deal with TAs in any of the blocks of flats they managed.

Variation of leases

Only two tenants, both living in purpose built blocks of flats were explicitly aware of their right to apply for a variation of the lease under the 1987 Act. One of these people was not aware that the provision covered the repair and maintenance of safety or security installations.

None of the landlords were aware of this provision in the 1987 Act, although a minority assumed that there must be a legal way of varying leases. By contrast, all of the managing agents were aware that leases could be varied, although with varying degrees of detail; they knew of the principle of the provision, but did not know, for example, that the calculation of service charges was included or that section 40 applied to leasehold houses under certain circumstances.

There was also some misunderstanding of the provision, some managing agents feeling that ALL parties had to be in agreement, for a deed of variation to be issued although the Act does provide rules for 'majority agreement'.

As very few people had used this part of the Act the comments received mainly concerned the principle of the Act and views about the procedures from a theoretical point of view. These will be discussed in the next chapter.

Appointment of a manager by the court

None of the tenants knew of this right under the 1987 Act although one said he suspected that there was such a legal entitlement. Very few landlords interviewed knew of this provision; one thought that tenants could probably initiate action in the court although was unsure about this. Managing agents were generally more familiar with this section of the Act; one was not aware; others did not realise that there were so many exclusions to the Act (e.g. leaseholders of houses, business tenants, etc.)

Views about the practical application of such a piece of legislation were very diverse; tenants viewed it as a 'last ditch' attempt when *"you've got to be in dire straights, haven't you?"*. They felt that while the legislation was laudable the need for expert witnesses and potentially lengthy court proceedings could mean that exercising one's rights under the Act could be very expensive. Most felt that they would prefer to explore other avenues before embarking on court proceedings to appoint a manager.

Landlords, in general, felt that the provision was *"fair"*, although commented that it was an avenue that should only be used as a last resort; they felt that it was a very complex and expensive way of solving landlord-tenant problems. They felt that situations should never get this far and that there should be less *"heavyweight"* methods of resolving such problems. In general, managing agents shared the landlord's views, commenting additionally that the Act should provide for managing agents to have a statutory 'right of reply'. Advisors were generally in agreement with these views.

Compulsory acquisition of the property

Knowledge about Part III (Compulsory acquisition) of the Act was extremely limited; only two leaseholders were aware of the principle of the provision; while all of the managing agents had heard of the provision they were rarely familiar with the grounds for taking court action or the process required to complete the compulsory purchase of the property. Only a minority of landlords were aware of this provision, in all cases, in outline only. It was common for respondents, particularly managing agents and landlords, to say that they were relatively unfamiliar with the provision because it is a piece of legislation that is only to be used in very extreme cases and which none of them had experienced. Consequently, they felt it important to stress that their views about the provision were likely to be rather superficial until they had either experienced the process themselves or had seen the results of action taken in the court. With this in mind, most managing agents and landlords, with a few conditions, felt that the provision was *"fair"*, although most maintained that they could see few scenarios where such a provision was required. Both tenants and the majority of advisors were generally in agreement with these views.

One managing agent and a few of the 'commercial advisors' felt that there was no need for this particular provision. One managing agent interpreted it as a 'right to buy', albeit under very unusual circumstances. He felt it was out of keeping with the spirit of the Act. He continues the argument:

> *"I think compulsory acquisition is unfair generally, but that's a personal view, but the fact you've got the remedy under Part II to appoint a receiver to look after the property properly, I would have thought was adequate remedy ... it's a nice threat to have perhaps."* (Managing agent, Paddington)

Right of first refusal

Awareness of Part I (Right of first refusal) of the 1987 Act was generally much higher than for other provisions. Indeed, many people associated the Landlord and Tenant Act 1987 with the right of first refusal. Around a third of the tenants had heard of the 'right of first refusal', the majority of whom were living in converted flats. A minority also had first hand experience of buying the freehold under the provisions of the Act.

It was clear that for many respondents the principle underlying this provision was totally new, others had been misinformed or were confused about their rights. A small number of people, for example, thought that the right of first refusal had been available for some years; others thought that they had a right to buy their freehold without it first being offered. It was clear that many had confused the right of council tenants to buy their rented flats with the legislation introduced under the Landlord and Tenant Act 1987.

Tenants, in general, were in agreement that the provision was fair and of benefit to them. They specified three main reasons: greater control over the management, maintenance and refurbishment of the building; greater control over the level and frequency of service charge demands; and the cessation of paying ground rent. There were also a number of critical comments, some related to the principle of the legislation, others to the procedures required by the Act. In terms of principle, while many felt that buying the freehold would be a solution to all their management problems, others were not so sure. As one woman, who had experience of purchasing the freehold prior to the commencement of the 1987 Act said:

> "... owning the freehold is not always the solution to management problems... when we bought, it was fine ... we all knew each other, were good friends ... and could talk about the management [of the block] .... Now, with new people moving in, it is really difficult to get things done, getting agreement for building works, and so on..." (Leaseholder, Brighton; self-managed conversion.)

In this instance, this respondent was living in a converted house that had a management committee that undertook the management of the property. She felt that, although fine in principle, buying the freehold could simply be swapping one set of problems for another; she conceded, however, that ultimately she had more control but felt that self-management was not always the most appropriate method of looking after a building.

Many tenants felt that the provision made owning the freehold a very complicated affair. Apart from the procedural requirements of the Act, which were often thought to be *"complicated"* or *"horrendous"* - and described in the next chapter - purchasing a freehold meant that a great deal of time, money and expertise were required. The necessity to collectively raise large sums of money (often millions of pounds), the need to set up a company to hold the freehold, arranging the management of the building, the time involved, and the legal expense likely to be incurred were considered by many to be prohibitive. *"There must be an easier way"* was frequently heard.

All of the managing agents were aware of the tenants' right of first refusal under the 1987 Act. A number of them had been involved in cases where the freehold was sold; in some instances the landlords had intended to sell or sold their interest without complying with the Act.

By contrast, few of the landlords interviewed had heard of this provision; only a minority had experience of selling their properties in recent years and in most cases complied with the legislation by offering the freehold to the tenants.

Managing agents' and landlords' views about this part of the Act (Part I) were sharply divided; comments related to both the principle of Part I of the Act as well as the procedures laid down. In terms of principle, there was a general feeling that the intentions behind the legislation were unclear.

Some felt that Part I was:

> *"an ill conceived way of buying the freehold ... pre-empting commonhold"* (Managing agent, Brighton)

Others saw Part I in terms of solving management problems:

> *"well, it's one way of getting the management under [the tenants'] control, but it's a jolly expensive way of doing it"* (Managing agent, Manchester)

Interestingly, a specialist advisor consulted at the outset of the study felt that the 'right of first refusal' was really a *"watered down right to buy"* ; a small number of the managing agents also saw Part I in these terms. One landlord (a builder) thought that the Act was too weak and felt that tenants should have a 'right to buy' their property.

Despite the confusion over the intentions of Part I of the 1987 Act, the majority of managing agents and landlords were in favour of the right of first refusal. There were a few dissenters to this view, both managing agents and landlords, all of whom felt that the provision would depress property prices:

> *"It's the landlord's property ... despite what leaseholders think, they have bought a lease with a time limit ... I see them as glorified renters ... the only difference is that they can sell their interest [lease] for a profit which a renter can't do ... landlords make little money out of ground rents so their business is about speculation .. if you have to offer to the tenants first you are effectively constraining the extent to which landlords can ask a speculative price ... tenants can't afford it, but companies can ... so this [Part I] pushes the prices down."* (Managing agent, Paddington)

One managing agent felt that the legislation was attempting to be 'retrospective'. He felt that the principle of owing a freehold was better, in terms of legal and management problems, than buying a lease. The question should be asked as to why leaseholders should now be entitled to buy the freehold - they bought a lease, he argued, knowing its implications;

> *"If you enter into a contract why should someone come along and change it without asking you?"*

However, he went on to argue that new properties should be sold as freehold - *"this is trying to impose a kind of solution on a system which has got a totally different philosophy"* - leasehold properties should, he argued, remain as they are.

3.4 Sources of information

The reported sources of information about the Landlord and Tenant Act 1987 were numerous, but were primarily of an informal nature. Tenants, in particular, had heard 'snippets' of information on the radio and from friends, and read occasional articles in national and local press. Those who had considered legal action were generally better informed - usually by their solicitors - although mention was often made of how difficult it had proved to find a solicitor who was familiar enough with the legislation and willing to handle such a case. Few tenants had seen and read the relevant booklets issued by the Department of the Environment. In this context, it was notable how many people said that they had become considerably better informed after the group discussions and many requested copies of the concepts boards (Appendix E) displayed during the discussions.

Landlords generally said that they relied upon their solicitors to inform them of the legislation; this was also true for managing agents, but in addition many subscribed to publications that provided synopses and/or interpretations of new legislation. Professional bodies, particularly the Royal Institute of Chartered Surveyors (RICS), were credited with providing information through their professional journal. The Estates Gazette was also an often mentioned source of legal information. In one instance a managing agent had attended a seminar about the 1987 Act convened by an enterprising local solicitor.

Overall, but with the general exception of managing agents, there was a feeling of being poorly informed about the legislation. Most of the tenants and landlords interviewed had little understanding of the Landlord and Tenant Act 1987, or its implications. Where there was awareness, knowledge was often vague and sometimes incorrect. We return to the issue of information - the type of information required and methods of dissemination - in Chapter 6.

3.5 Summary

There was a marked lack of awareness about the Landlord and Tenant Act 1987 and its provisions and implications. Tenants, in particular, were likely to be the least well informed, managing agents the most comprehensively informed. A number of the landlords were not aware of their duties under the Act; some were not complying through ignorance on their part, others were complying but only because their practices happened to be in accord with the Act's provisions and not through any vigilance on their part.

Although the 1987 Act applies to management companies run by tenants in the same way as it does to managing agents and landlords, it was notable that, in general, markedly little awareness of the Act's provisions was shown by this group of respondents.

A wide range of views were expressed about the Act's provisions; the level of comment tended to be related to the relevance of the provision to an individual's problems. Consequently, sections relating to service charges, information to be provided about the landlord, and the right of first refusal tended to receive most comment.

Overall, the 1987 Act was viewed as being useful in part (particularly the three sections just mentioned) whilst other sections were seen as useable only in extreme cases (for example, appointment of a manager and compulsory acquisition).

Many comments concerning the efficacy of the Act and the 'fine detail' of the provisions were received. Three general themes emerged as central to the Act's usefulness. First, there was a considerable weight of opinion that indicated that the Act's procedures were often cumbersome, yet poorly defined. Second, court action as a means of enforcing the Act's provisions was seen as totally inappropriate; the delays involved in taking court action and the expense incurred were seen as prohibitive and only likely to be available to the very wealthy. Third, tenants in particular, felt that the Act *"lacked teeth"*. In instances were landlords or managing agents did not comply with the law they felt that in addition to taking legal action against them, financial penalties should be built into the Act as a means of persuading landlords to comply with the Act.

Chapter 4

Experiences and Views of the Landlord and Tenant Act 1987

In the previous chapter it was shown that the principle of the 1987 Act was generally acknowledged to be of benefit in moderating the relationship between landlords and tenants. However, there were many reservations expressed about the intentions of the Act and the way in which the legislation would work in practice. In this chapter we consider the Act's provisions in the light of people's experiences of using them. We review respondents' experiences of using the legislation; the circumstances under which they have done so and consider the reasons why people decide against taking action under the 1987 Act.

Very few of those respondents taking part in the first stage of the study had experience of using the 1987 Act (Appendix B - Contact and approach). However, many respondents without direct experience had views about the Act's provisions; a number of the advisors and solicitors interviewed in the study fell into this category. In addition to discussing people's experience of using the Act we therefore provide a critical commentary of each of the individual provisions based on interviews carried out with all the respondents from both stages of the study.

The number of respondents in the sample who had used the provisions of the 1987 Act, or considered their use was, fairly small. Table 4.1 provides a summary of this information. This table is provided purely as a way of describing the sample of respondents. It does not provide any statistical evidence of usage of the Act's provisions.

4.1 Information to be furnished to tenants (Part VI)

In this section we consider respondents' views and experiences of this part of the legislation. Many concerns were raised about the practicalities of implementing this part (VI) of the Act. Overall, three main issues emerged: difficulties with identifying and contacting the landlord, using the Land Register, and general limitations of the legislation. We begin first with respondents' views and experiences.

Views and experiences

Most respondents were in agreement that it was *"fair"* to know who the landlord was and to be able to contact them when necessary. Compliance with sections 47 and 48[1] generally seemed to be high; all of the managing agents and most of the landlords said that they provided a contact address and most of the tenants knew the name and address of their landlord. There were, however, a small number of tenants who did not know the identity of their landlord and had been unable to find out. None of the tenants had withheld service charge payments for non-compliance with section 47.

---

[1] Landlord's name and address to be contained in demands for rent, etc., and notification by landlord of address for service of notices, respectively.

Table 4.1 Tenants' use, or considered use, of the provisions contained in the Landlord and Tenant Act 1987

Provision	No of respondents making use of provision	No of respondents who had considered, but not used, the provision
Information to be furnished to tenants		
Withholding payment[1]	-	-
Searching Land Register	4	-
Service charges		
Challenging service charge demand	12	-
Inspecting receipts	2	-
Consultation about building works		
Challenging estimates	6	-
Insurance of the property		
Challenging landlord's decisions	1	-
Variation of lease	2	3
Appointment of manager by the court	2	1
Compulsory acquisition	-	1[2]
Right of first refusal		
Right conferred, freehold purchased	8	
freehold not purchased	3	
Right not conferred, freehold purchased	1	
freehold not purchased	4	

[1] A number of tenants had withheld part, or all, of the service charge for other reasons, such as disputes over service charge demands, poor quality works, etc.

[2] Pending expiry of the three year time limit imposed under Part II (Appointment of managers) of the Act.

Managing agents and landlords were largely in agreement that this provision was acceptable, although some thought that it was limited in its usefulness. Some of the managing agents said that although they complied with the law, their clients (landlords) were not happy with such an arrangement, for two main reasons. First, there was a tendency for tenants to get confused about who was dealing with the management of the property and send documents and service charge payments to the landlords rather than their agent. More importantly, landlords were not pleased to *"receive calls in the middle of the night to fix a hole in my roof"* from tenants when it was the managing agents' responsibility to do so. A Brighton landlord describes one of his experiences:

> *"... the worst thing I ever had with a leaseholder, and it seems to be with leaseholders more than tenants, tenants always give you time, leaseholders won't. I think the worst was a half past one phone call in the morning, when a young lady got back from a club, and she walked in to find that her - that she had no hot water from her electric water heater. I don't think it was anything to do with me, something on the thermostat had gone. Half past one in the morning. I mean, would you take a phone call then?"* (Landlord, Brighton)

Difficulties with identifying and contacting the landlord

This part of the Act is intended to provide a facility for tenants to make contact and have a dialogue with the landlord, where necessary. Yet it is possible for the landlord to comply with the legislation while the tenant still remains unable to engage the landlord in discussion. This can occur because of the following reasons:

- Although a tenant may have the landlords' name and address, the landlord may either refuse to reply, or refer the tenant to the managing agent;

- Some landlords give a Post Office Box number as a contact address, others use accommodation addresses. In the event of no reply to letters, the tenants are unable to pursue the matter any further;

- Landlords can, and do, give false names and addresses;

- Many people felt that the biggest problem lay with non-resident landlords who were out of the jurisdiction of the English courts.

Use of the Land Register

Four people had used the Land Register as a means of tracing their landlord, although with limited success. For example, some people found that their property was registered in a name that turned out not to be the landlord. This was thought to occur either because the landlord did not register the property or failed to notify the Land Register on transfer of ownership. In other instances, while a tenant had been able to find the landlord's name and address from the Land Register, it was of little value - the landlord had registered himself as living in the house which he had leased to the tenant.

Additionally, where the property is registered in the name of a company, it was often said by advisors and solicitors to be very difficult to identify the ultimate parent (or holding) company.

Limitations of Part VI of the 1987 Act

Difficulties with identifying and contacting the landlord were often thought to be due to deficiencies with the legislation. What is the point, many people argued, of having a contact address if it is likely to be *"worthless"* and not legally enforceable? A number of tenants and advisors thought this Part of the Act to be *"window dressing"* and of little use in cases where the landlord did not want to be identified and contacted.

A number of solutions were suggested. Some of the respondents called for a formal register of landlords, policed by a professional body. Those who did not register, it was felt, should be considered to be operating illegally. In a number of instances this was likened to the way in which doctors register with their professional body for which the penalty for malpractice is being 'struck off'. Others endorsed different solutions. Some felt that the right to withhold service charge payments should be extended to rent and ground rent, as this was thought to provide more of a 'penalty' to landlords as it denied them their income. However, it was also pointed out that ground rents are often quite small and can be negligible in terms of a landlords' income. Others felt that landlords should be given a **specified** time limit in which to reply to correspondence. Non-compliance should result in a financial penalty for the landlord.

A number of people (primarily tenants and advisors) advocated that Part VI of the Act should be strengthened by adding financial penalties for non-compliance. This was because ultimately there was a feeling that while the spirit of the provision was beneficial, the principle of withholding service charges as a means of obtaining the landlord's name and address was limited in scope and, at times, counter-productive. For example, as one managing agent said:

> "... withholding the service charge doesn't make all that much difference as if they don't pay how does the [managing] agent run the place."

and a tenant conceded:

> "At the end of the day you're going to have to pay the service charge anyway so it isn't of any benefit."

Sometimes penalties per se were not seen as a panacea, but as a useful bargaining tool:

> "Often when they withhold their payment that causes other problems. That's the difficulty. I'm always loathe to advise people to withhold [payment], even when it's very clearly a right open to them. Because that's the one thing that's going to get a landlord riled and nasty and we don't like to encourage that. Penalties are the same, but they're both useful .... If you've got a couple of legally enforceable threats up your sleeve it can do wonders." (Croydon, Advisor)

Nevertheless, penalties were thought to be useful in encouraging landlords to comply with the legislation. In addition, to be consistent with the 1985 Act, the 1987 Act should, it was thought, be amended to include financial penalties for non-compliance. An advisor takes up the story:

> "... the '85 Act is usually more useful in a sense. Because the '85 Act actually contains an offence for not providing a mailing address, whereas the '87 Act doesn't actually contain an offence..... it doesn't give us any powers so we normally use the '85 Act ..... the limitation there is that the '85 Act only applies to weekly tenants, so if we get a monthly tenant who's landlord's name and address isn't shown we have to rely on the '87 Act. But it's less useful, I mean, it carries less weight because they can withhold their payment but we can't threaten prosecution ... if we're going to be consistent it [withholding name and address] should be an offence, rather than just saying payment shouldn't be payable." (Croydon, Advisor)

Managing agents and landlords were almost universally averse to the notion of including financial penalties for non-compliance into this part of the Act.

People who rent their accommodation, but who do not pay a variable service charge were thought to be the least likely to benefit from this section of the Act. While renters should have a rent book in which the landlord's name and address should appear, this is not always the case, as some advisors told us. While such cases were thought to be few in number, it was felt by some advisors that the Act should be extended to cover people who rent their accommodation but who do not pay a variable service charge.

4.2 Service charges (Section 41, Schedule 2)

In general service charges and the issue of accounting and consultation were the most incendiary issues. Many tenants had experienced a problem or had some negative views about how services in their block of flats were paid for. A number of issues arose concerning the calculation of service charges, challenging the sums demanded, accounting procedures, and inspecting receipts.

Calculation of service charges

Under the 1987 Act, tenants have the right to know how service charges are calculated, to inspect receipts, and to 'challenge' sums demanded. Few people in this study were consulted about the service charges required for the year. In general, respondents simply received a demand for service charges without any consultation. Many were very unhappy about this and felt that there should be a legal obligation for managing agents and landlords to discuss, face to face, the service charge demand. Where this had occurred, in a small number of cases, most were pleased with the outcome.

Respondents said that there were three main problems arising out of the service charge demands they received; paying for non-existent services; the provision of too many services; and rapidly escalating service charge demands. We discuss each of these in turn.

There was a general feeling amongst many of the tenants that the service charges they paid were too high for the level of service provided. For example, many tenants said that they were living in blocks of flats that had been neglected, in terms of maintenance, often for considerable lengths of time, or else they had facilities that were not working (entry-phone and security systems were often mentioned in this context). In such cases, many were charged for these services plus a management fee that they considered was not commensurate with the service provided.

By contrast, others felt that the managing agents and landlords were providing too many services that were not required by the tenants - landscaping, re-roofing and 'over-decorating' the common parts of the building were often mentioned.

Overspending and underspending were considered by tenants in much the same way - in both cases managing agents, in particular, were seen as *"making money out of the tenants"*. In the former case, tenants felt that the agents were taking a management fee whilst providing an inadequate, and in some cases, a non-existent service. In others, the agents were perceived to be able to make money on services provided. This was because of the way the agent's fees were calculated. Where the fee was based on a percentage of the turnover of the service charge account, then it was thought by tenants that managing agents had a vested interest in providing high levels of services, often at premium rates, as this would inflate the management fee. The issue of management fees was raised a number of times; we discuss the issue more fully in Chapter 6.

Many tenants were concerned that the service charges were increasing far too rapidly. Most understood that service charges were likely to increase because of inflation and the rising costs of the services required. Most accepted that if they were paying in advance there would need to be a contingency element in their payment to cover rising costs. However, there was a general feeling amongst tenants that managing agents and landlords should show precisely how this contingency element is calculated. Similarly, some felt that the inflation element in the service charge account was often excessive, respondents quoting contingencies of 25% - 50% to cover the increased costs, which they felt was unrealistic.

Challenging service charge demands

The 1987 Act provides for tenants to 'challenge' sums demanded. In total, 12 tenants had challenged the service charge demands in the sense that the 1987 Act allows it. Most people felt that they had three courses of action: they could write to the managing agent or landlord to challenge the level of demand (12 instances); they could withhold either all, or part, of the service charge money until the building was properly maintained (8 instances), or they could contest the level of the demand in court (3 instances).

Challenging the demand with the managing agent was mostly found to be an inadequate way of resolving disputes over service charges:

> "We have challenged the service charges and they've just written over and over again and won't change it." (Paddington leaseholder - converted house in three flats requiring £23,000 of work before building society would approve purchase of the freehold by the leaseholder.)

> "... they [landlord and managing agent] just won't talk about it. We know there are items in the [service charge] account that are wrong, but they refuse to see us." (Paddington, Leaseholder)

Although not a provision in the 1987 Act, others had withheld all, or part of, their service charge money. Typically, where this had happened tenants were sued by the landlord for non-payment. In some instances, the threat of court action resulted in tenants paying the outstanding service charge. A Brighton leaseholder takes up the story:

> ".. things were pretty bad for the first couple of years... it wasn't awful but the building obviously needed work doing to it, work that had been promised. For example, they promised an entry phone when I bought the lease and they didn't put it in, but they charged rent for it! ... It was outstanding and we were paying for it, so I stopped paying... I don't know how much the rent was a year but it wasn't enough to take anybody to court .... I withheld my maintenance but at the end of the day they [the managing agents] didn't care. They would just send threatening letters and eventually I gave up ... they were not doing what they claimed to be doing, they were charging for all sorts of things that they shouldn't have been. But not significant amounts that it was worth the enormous hassle and expense of getting into litigation."

In another instance, a leaseholder of a converted flat in Croydon had withheld the service charge payment because the managing agents were said to have neglected the property for over two years. The leaseholder decided to make an offer for the freehold, and a bargain was struck with the landlord, but only on condition that the outstanding service charge monies were paid to the managing agent. In this instance the leaseholder was convinced, though did not have sufficient proof, that the landlord and the managing agent were either the same company or they had mutual business interests. Again, it was not felt worthwhile to start legal proceedings - a solicitor had advised that the cost of court action could easily outweigh the outstanding service charge debt of £2,000.

The three people who had instigated court action were rarely satisfied with the outcome. For example, a Paddington leaseholder took the managing agents to court for overcharging and for lack of services. He felt that with hindsight court action was not the best route to have taken:

> "... we have never ever had any work done in this block, be it minor or major, that was not a complete and utter disaster... the work has been shoddy, everything has been done again and redone again. It's been impossible to prove against their arguments that it didn't fall apart six weeks later because of some outside element .... there has never ever been a winter where everybody has had heating ... they spend thousands on trying to get it working properly. It should be under guarantee but they find some excuse.

...last year we had no cleaning service for six months. They continued to charge ... we had no resident porter for last year but we're still paying agency fees and rent on his flat... they had the block rewired two years ago, it's still never been certified as being satisfactory ... we did fight and put one case together. We won. But I think it was the wrong way to go about it... in the end it was costing too much money ... the agents would start the work, which would halt the court action, and then stop [the work] again so we had to start [court action] all over again .... I think the way now I've decided to go about it is to stop paying. If they think they have a strong enough case let them sue us."

Overwhelmingly, leaseholders felt that the 1987 legislation did little to strengthen their rights in terms of seeking redress for poor quality service. The right to 'challenge' was said to be good in principle, but in practice it was a provision that was simply ignored by some landlords and managing agents. Leaseholders and many of the advisors felt that this section of the Act needed considerable strengthening. A number of suggestions were made: managing agents and landlords should provide written documentation in support of the service charge demand; where demands were challenged, written replies should be made compulsory; a simple, cheap method of arbitration should be available that does not involve court action.

Managing agents and landlords varied in their views. Many felt that situations should never be allowed to progress to such a state. They felt that this was 'bad management' and should never occur. A number of them had adopted strategies to 'head off' such a deterioration in managing agent-tenant relations (Chapter 2). Others, however, were less concerned: *"they can take me to court all they like"* said one managing agent.

One issue that did unite the views of managing agents and landlords was over recovering overdue service charges. Most felt that there should be a mechanism by which this could be accomplished both speedily and without too much expense.

Service charge accounts

In this section we discuss the issue of service charge accounts in terms of their availability and their format.

Obtaining a service
charge account

For some tenants, obtaining a service charge account was said to be a major problem. A small number of tenants had continuously requested an end of year statement of account from their managing agents and landlords. Most expressed considerable anger about this but felt that the solution of legal action was not very appropriate. Typical comments were:

"they [managing agents] just ignore you... and it's too expensive to go to court"

"why should I pay good money [to go to court] to get something that is my right anyway"

A Brighton leaseholder speaks from her experience:

"Failure to produce service charge accounts can be another problem. Although such default is, under the Landlord and Tenant Act 1985, a criminal offence, if tenants take their landlord to court they incur legal expenses.

Despite being awarded costs against the landlord, they may still have difficulty in enforcing judgement." (Our emphasis)

Overwhelmingly, tenants felt that the legislation, although correct in principle did little to help them when faced with managing agents and landlords who refused to comply with the law. Court action was almost universally opposed on three grounds. The first was cost, which many felt they would not be able to recoup in full; second, the delays involved in taking court action; and third, recourse to legal action was often felt to be a 'heavy-handed' solution to an essentially simple problem.

The format of service charge accounts

Many tenants were not happy with the information they were provided with that related to how the service charge was spent. In general, this was for two main reasons: complicated or technical formats, and lack of detail.

Many tenants received a 'balance sheet' at the end of the year. While welcoming the information, many said that they were not familiar with company accounts and could make little sense of the information. Again, there were a variety of views expressed about the format of service charge accounts. Some people did want a formal balance sheet, while others required a less technical presentation. In general, however, people said that they required an account statement that was simple to understand, that did not use technical language and perhaps provided a commentary on the items of expenditure. Few had asked for such information, in part because they felt that there were more pressing issues to discuss with managing agents and in part because they felt that they would be *"charged more for the privilege of knowing what they [the managing agents] did with my money"*.

In many cases the accounts provided were felt to be insufficiently detailed for a full understanding of how the money had been used. One tenant mentioned that she had an entry on her service charge account headed 'security'. She felt that this was insufficiently detailed. After pressing the managing agents for some months she found that this item included a maintenance payment for the entry-phone system (which had not worked for the previous year), the building's insurance and the replacement of light bulbs in the common entrance way.

This is an example of just one of the many tenants that felt that every item of expenditure should be detailed on the service charge account. A small number of people disagreed and were happy with 'general' accounts. Although the issue can not be resolved here, from our discussions it emerged that tenants were very keen that there should be guidelines - many said 'enforceable guidelines' - as to the nature and composition of service charge accounts.

Accounts were of concern to managing agents and landlords too:

"I produce proper maintenance accounts with all the information on it... The one thing I believe is when you produce a maintenance account, you should carry over the position from the previous year and take something forward for the future. Now a lot of the maintenance accounts I see in this town are just a cloud of figures and leaseholders are supposed to understand what the position is. And it's not easy. I mean, when I buy freeholds I get maintenance accounts in, I look at them and read them through and I can't understand them. And I'm producing them for my properties! But I mean, to me, it's a simple income, expenditure and reserve situation. There is the only three items that come into it basically. As long as you show it properly, in some form of table then I think everybody should be able to understand it. For

example, what you had at the start of the year plus (a) which is your income [from service charges and interest], less (b) which is your expenditure, plus (c) if there's a reserve built up for major expenditure, equals (d). But unfortunately, a lot of what I see [maintenance accounts] are not that straightforward at all." (Landlord, Brighton)

Many managing agents and landlords said that they were keen to provide the information required by tenants, provided that the cost of producing the information could be adequately reflected in the management fee. Most felt that guidelines as to the form and content of service charge accounts would be useful, while others felt that it should be an issue resolved with the tenants themselves. Most did not feel the need for statutory guidelines.

An issue that was raised by a small number of tenants was that managing and accounting should be separated to avoid conflicts of interest and potential malpractice. It was felt, therefore, that either managing agents should manage the building and a separate firm of accountants should take care of the accounts, or that managing agents should retain the accounting function but that the end of year service charge accounts should be independently audited. Tenants were divided in their views over this. For those who had considered this option, most raised objections over the cost. However, two tenants taking part in the second stage of the study, who had been involved in purchasing the freehold, had adopted such a practice. Collectively, the tenants had appointed managing agents to manage the building and separate accountants to handle the service charge accounts. Although a more expensive option they felt that it gave them total control over how the service charge money had been spent - they were very happy with this arrangement. In general, landlords and their agents felt that this practice was unnecessary. Some felt, however, that an independent audit, providing it was paid for by the tenants, would be advantageous.

Inspecting receipts

Most of the tenants felt that the right to inspect receipts was a valuable one although only two respondents had exercised their right to do so.

Managing agents and landlords felt that while the principle of tenants having the right to inspect receipts was correct, it was unnecessarily burdensome. Two managing agents, had experience of this. With hindsight both felt that this was a potentially very expensive process. One had a policy of charging a fee to cover the photocopying process. The other had, on this occasion, absorbed the costs, but felt that in future the staff time involved in locating the relevant information would be charged to the service charge account. Most of the managing agents and landlords agreed that any costs incurred should be recouped from the service charge account. One managing agent felt that the procedures specified in the 1987 Act put them in a difficult position. He explains:

".. the right to look at vouchers; it says here the landlord can not charge you, fine, that's quite right, but it [the 1987 Act] goes on to say the landlord can have regard to the cost of providing the facilities and add it to his costs of management, which is the same thing. Fine, Joe Smith comes in, I can't give him a bill for £300 because looking at vouchers isn't chargeable ... the last time we did this they were here a full day and we charged down £350 [to the service charge account] ... that was just our time, it took a senior accounts person all day long, plus we have to make available the facilities to sit the person down and everything else, but reading this it says the landlords can't charge for this cost. I think that's unfair because all the lessees pay for this if only one wants it ... the person who wants it should be charged and its' up

41

to them to arrange reimbursement from the other lessees ... otherwise it pushes my fees higher and makes me look bad." (Managing agent, Paddington)

Overview

The issue of service charges was raised many times during the interviews by all parties. The problem arises as a number of respondents argued, because there is an inherent distrust between tenants and the managing agents when it comes to money. Regulating the management profession, introducing legally enforceable guidelines and ensuring that service charge provisions are adequately described in leases were some suggested solutions to these problems. (These are described more fully in Chapter 6). Separating the roles of management and the accounting, or by making it a statutory requirement to have service charge accounts independently audited would, it was also argued, alleviate many of the problems associated with leasehold management.

A rather more radical suggestion came from one of the solicitors in the study:

"In my experience, when acting for lessees, the main problems have either been over charging in relation to service or maintenance charges on the one hand, or failure to repair or manage adequately on the other hand. Although it is possible to tinker with these problems by amending existing legislation such as the 1987 Act or the service charge provision in the 1985 Act, essentially they arise from the unsatisfactory nature of leasehold title. It is very easy for conflicts of interest to arise between freeholders who merely have one kind of financial interest and lessees who have not only a different financial interest, but also who actually live in the premises. Although the Law Commission's commonhold proposals will not guarantee the resolution of these problems in all cases, I do believe that the introduction of a commonhold system, with the possibility of compulsion where freeholders are reluctant to transfer ownership to a commonhold association, is the best solution."

However, it is very clear that the present arrangements for service charges are less than adequate on four counts; the presentation of service charge accounts; the need for audited service charge accounts; the method of calculating service charge demands due in advance; and the methods by which a person can challenge the service charge accounts. It was felt by the majority of tenants and some of the managing agents and landlords that guidelines were essential. Tenants were more likely to feel that such guidelines should be legally enforceable.

4.3 Consultation about building works (Section 41, Schedule 2)

A large number of issues were raised under the ambit of consultation about building works. These generally fell into one of five categories: consultation over the selection of estimates, challenging estimates; resolving disputes about the quality of work done; consultation thresholds; and the rights of Tenants' Associations.

Consultation over the selection of estimates

Most of the managing agents indicated that they provided estimates of building work for the tenants' approval. Where requested, they would also entertain estimates provided by the tenants themselves. However, tenants felt that their estimates were *"usually binned"*, whilst one managing agent said

"I look at it like this. It is the freeholder's property and we are his agent... our responsibilities lie with the freeholder ... we feel that it is important to take account of the leaseholders' views, but ultimately we are acting for the

leaseholder and we have a responsibility to see that his investment is protected ... and that doesn't meantaking the cheapest quote." (Landlord, Brighton)

There was a general feeling amongst the managing agents in particular that the consultation procedures, although correct in principle had the effect of delaying, often essential, repairs. *"There is always one tenant who disagrees with the estimates"* was a common retort. Many said that the delay could increase the cost of the maintenance in the long term. They felt that there were two areas that were left open for interpretation and in need of clarification. First, one managing agent interpreted the 1987 Act as requiring *"100% approval from residents"*. However, others felt that a majority decision was acceptable and operated on that principle. Secondly, there was some discussion about the length of time that 'consultation' should take. Most waited for a *"reasonable"* time; one managing agent stated specifically that they *"give one month to consider the proposal and to get their [the tenants] own estimates"*. Most felt that a 'reasonable' time for consultation could be arrived at *"by commonsense"*. The process of consultation, however, was felt to be poorly specified in the Act and consequently open to interpretation - the need for guidelines to be issued was frequently mentioned.

In some cases, managing agents were said to arrange for new estimates to be provided. In others, tenants were asked to provide new estimates. However, in this latter case, where the estimated was accepted, managing agents were said to absolve all responsibility over claims of poor quality work. One managing agent sums up his method:

> *"... serve a section 146 notice... the tenants can serve counter notice under the 1938 Leasehold Repairs Act ... tenants are given the opportunity to carry out repairs within a certain time. If they don't we proceed with the work and recover the costs and damages later on, through the Court if necessary."*

However, tenants, in particular felt that there were a number of landlords and managing agents who manipulated the 'consultation' requirements of the 1987 Act to their own advantage. Where this occurred, it was felt that managing agents did this for one of two reasons: first, they had an interest in, or an association with a particular building firm; second, where they charged a percentage of the works carried out as a management fee, it was to their advantage to inflate the cost of building works. A number of methods for avoiding consultation were described:

* the managing agent accepts the lowest tender and then finds that 'out of specification' works need to be carried out. In some instances this doubled the original estimate;

* some managing agents consistently refuse to use any other builder or trade person than those they had selected themselves;

* tenants' estimates are not available for use;

> *"They do [managing agents] everything correctly, or so it seems. They ask us if we want to nominate anybody to tender for the work. We say yes, our request for quotes go out. They get lost in the post. Our builders say they weren't given enough time to quote. Something always goes wrong. There's always some funny business."* (Paddington, Leaseholder)

* inappropriate contracts are entered into

"They [managing agents] didn't really seem to let appropriate contracts. The contract was let [for roofing and exterior repairs] in the winter time ... within the tender period there was the Christmas period ... they claimed time for bad, inclement weather, which they added onto the bill.s" (Paddington, Leaseholder)

Challenging estimates

Only a small number of tenants interviewed had challenged building specifications and costs. Indeed, it was only a few who had experienced major building works. Nevertheless, many felt that there were potential difficulties with challenging estimates because of the vagueness surrounding words such as 'entitled' and 'challenge' which appear in the legislation. Although the spirit of the law may provide for the facility to challenge estimates, many felt that this could be avoided in practice; the legislation was felt to be potentially ineffective because the landlord or managing agent could overrule the tenants' views.

Where there were disputes about the estimates provided, respondents, in general, felt that the Act did little to provide any form of resolution. Two suggestions were put forward. First, there was a considerable body of opinion indicating that managing agents and landlords should be legally required to give written reasons as to why the tenants' estimates had been rejected, prior to any works being carried out. Second, while it was accepted that recourse to court action was possible, most felt that this was a potentially expensive and cumbersome way of resolving the problem; the notion of an independent arbitrator whose decision was legally binding was often mentioned in this context.

Indeed, a small number of tenants had taken legal action over estimates for building works, with varying degrees of success. In the following example the managing agents had initially *"dragged their heels"* over essential repairs. The consequence was that the estimate dramatically increased which the leaseholder was now contesting. Although his court action was successful he found that he was considerably out of pocket because he had not been able to recoup all of his costs. In this instance, a Brighton leaseholder had advised his agents that corrective action was needed to check the development of dry rot in the basement. The agents refused to sanction the works. After a year and numerous delays, the dry rot had spread and the managing agents were now demanding more money to complete the job (the cost had increased from £60,000 to £135,000, split across 6 people). The court found in the leaseholders favour and ordered that the work be carried out. However, because the cost of building works had doubled in this time, the respondent felt entitled to claim compensation from the managing agent - the managing agents offered £2,500 - whereas the increase in cost was nearer £15,000. Because there is also a dispute about who is liable for the work, the managing agent or the landlord, there is also some doubt as to whether this respondent will be able to recoup all of his litigation costs.

Resolving disputes about poor quality work

Generally, across the whole sample of respondents there was a view that better control was needed over the quality of building works:

"I think there should be something done about builders. I don't employ bad ones, I hope. If I do [have a problem], I go back, I go back on the builders, but I haven't really had any great necessity, I mean, there's been a few little things. But a lot of cowboys are used by managing agents, and I think there should be stricter control over quality. I don't really think there's control over the building game". (Landlord, Brighton)

In cases of poor quality building works, tenants felt that their legal redress was very limited. Because few were willing to start court proceedings, either because of the cost or the unpredictable nature of the outcome, those in this situation had resorted to withholding their service charge payments. As one Brighton leaseholder points out, this action is in breach of the tenants' lease and does not always guarantee success.

> *"Provided that landlords or their managing agents are prepared to negotiate disputes can often be satisfactorily resolved. Unfortunately some landlords and/or their managing agents have no intention of negotiating. Where tenants who dispute the service charge have withheld part of the amount demanded, thus being technically in breach of the term of their lease, the landlord/managing agent may issue a notice under Section 146, Law of Property Act 1925, requiring payment of the outstanding amount, failing which application will be made to the court for forfeiture of the lease. Tenants receiving this notice may decide to pay the disputed amount rather than face the expense and worry of a court action."*

A number of tenants argued that currently the onus was on them to prove whether the quality of work had been carried out to an acceptable standard. Where they had provided the accepted estimate or had commissioned the work themselves, this they felt was fair. However, where this was not the case, they felt that in cases of dispute it was the managing agents' or landlords' responsibility to demonstrate that the work was adequately carried out. In some instances, neither managing agents or landlords agreed. Most of the tenants felt that the 1987 Act gave no help at all in addressing difficulties where disputes over quality of work occurred.

A small number of tenants had taken legal action over the quality of building works. For example, one tenant talked about a major refurbishment program carried out on a converted mansion block consisting of eight flats had been in excess of one million pounds. The tenants were prepared for the cost of the works but were bitter about the quality of the work carried out. The cost of taking legal action was £90,000. They had been granted only £70,000 in costs so they were out of pocket by £20,000. At the time of interview they were having difficulty in recovering these costs.

> *"How often are you going to do this and take them to court"* this tenant argued.

In terms of seeking compensation for poor quality work most managing agents recognised that it was not worth taking court action unless the sums involved were substantial - building works of one hundred thousand pounds, for example, was mentioned by one landlord. Their solution was to ask the contractor to put the problem right - most managing agents and landlords had 'preferred' contractors whose work they felt met the required standards - and if their wishes were not carried out then that contractor would not be used again.

Two issues strongly emerge from this discussion. First, inadequate control over the quality of building works, and second a general feeling that all those concerned attempted to deny responsibility for taking corrective action. For example, managing agents felt it was their duty to ensure the quality of the work carried out, and some were willing to take corrective action, but only if any expenses incurred could be charged to the maintenance account. Yet other agents felt that it was not their responsibility, but the landlords', with whom they had their contract. Landlords, in general, did not believe it was their responsibility where the work had been sanctioned by their agent.

A general issue concerning consultation thresholds was raised. It was thought that the present limits (£1,000 or £50 per dwelling) were too low and should be raised; they should also be updated annually in line with either the Retail Price Index or an index of building costs.

One managing agent also felt that the process of establishing whether consultation should take place had been unnecessarily complicated by the 1987 Act. In the past the decision to consult had been based on the number of flats in the block, whereas now it was based on the number of qualifying flats (ie flats held on long leases). This, it was felt, was a minor issue, but nevertheless an unnecessary complication.

A number of respondents, tenants and managing agents indicated that while consultation thresholds were fine in practice they were easy to circumvent. The way that some managing agents had found to do this was to split the building works into a number of discrete pieces of work that could be carried out at regular intervals, but which fell below the threshold for consultation. The legislation, it was felt, could be tightened by requiring that the consultation thresholds should refer to the service charge period (usually a year). Any work that took the cumulative cost of works for that period over a specified threshold (say £2,000) should require consultation to occur.

The rights of Tenants' Associations

While Tenants' Associations were pleased to be entitled to detailed building work specifications an issue arose over the fairness of this. Although none of the tenants were aware of this provision, in discussion most felt that it was an unfair provision. After all, they argued, tenants pay the service charge, why should only TAs be entitled to a detailed specification? It was an anomaly that most felt should be corrected.

4.4 Holding service charge money in trust (Section 42)

In this section, we deal with two specific issues: interpretations of how money should be held under Section 42 of the 1987 Act; and the issue of paying and charging interest to service charge accounts.

Almost all tenants felt that the 1987 Act's provision of holding service charge payments in trust was beneficial, although few were really convinced that this was an adequate form of protection; most felt that the money should be held separately from the managing agents or landlord's company money and should be protected in instances of insolvency. Most felt that a separate account was the most satisfactory and reassuring way of dealing with this.

Managing agents, in particular, felt that this provision was a 'grey area' in the Act, giving rise to difficulties of interpretation. Two questions consistently arose: *"How should service charge payments be held?"* and *"Are sinking funds covered by section 42 of the 1987 Act?"* Most had taken guidance, either from their solicitors, their professional bodies or the Department of the Environment; many felt uneasy at the guidance they had been given and hoped that the Department of the Environment would publish guidance notes on this issue.

> *"We have been to counsel, we have also received, unsolicited, four opinions from members [of professional body] who have been to counsel, and they're all different, most of them, quite a number have said you need separate funds in separate bank accounts."* (Managing agent, Paddington)

Most of the managing agents held service charge payments in a single *"capital expenditure/repairs"* fund using accounting methods to identify the relevant monies attributable to each of the properties under their management. The majority of landlords adopted the same procedure, although not generally as a result of the 1987 Act - this was something they said they had always done. One, however, used a separate bank account for each property; another had unwittingly fallen foul of the legislation by placing all the service charge money into 'the company account'. They were not able to identify the money accruing to each property "*without considerable difficulty*".

Overall, most of the landlords and managing agents felt that the identification of service charge money by accounting procedures was the most sensible and cost effective method, although all agreed that this money should be held separately from the company's day-to-day working capital.

One managing agent raised two very specific queries about this section of the Act. First, he felt that the Act's intentions were unclear as to whether Section 42 intended service charge money to be held in a trust fund. Although he had taken advice, he felt that the explanation lacked clarity. For example:

> "*Section 42 deals with the creation of trust funds ... we went to the Department of the Environment and they said well we think it means this [it operates like a trust] and we said well surely, if you've set up a trust, most trusts have a trustee which have rules, surely ... where are the rules. All it says is you have a trust fund, and then they said, oh well the Law Society, they hold clients money in trust, how do they get by. Well they have a blind spot, the whole investment of the Law Society is by statute which gives them certain power, much more, for example, than the RICS.*" (Managing agent, Paddington)

Second, he also felt that the holding of money in trust in the way the 1987 Act specifies does not provide adequate protection against fraud or theft. Neither, in his view, does it extend existing law to any great degree. He outlines his views:

> "*If the landlord goes into liquidation, or runs away, eventually a receiver steps in and the receiver must dispose of the property. Let's say he absconds with £250,000 of service charge money. That is a burden to the new purchaser. Now he will now know that the resource fund of £250,000 managed to find its way into a suitcase to Rio, so when he looks at the price he will pay for that block, he will say I've got a deficit of £250,000 - to make up the reserve fund because, you know, you won't get it from the lessees again ... the law of assignment of a freehold interest is that the new owner steps into the obligations and benefits of the previous owner, good and bad. Therefore, he will pay at a price that would have reflected that the reserve fund went walkies.... Why was this [Section 42] necessary to protect this money ... the money is still protected by the law of assignment of freehold interests ... it's no protection from dishonesty ... so how does Section 42 extend what we already have under the law of assignment.*"

Paying interest on service charge accounts

An issue that was often raised in the context of the way in which service charge payments, and particularly long-term 'sinking funds' are held was whether interest should be paid to tenants.

Some managing agents did place money into interest earning accounts and allocated the interest to the tenants. In the majority of cases this tended to be for long-term 'sinking fund' money; only a very small number of tenants in the study contributed to sinking funds, usually because there was no provision to operate such funds in the lease. Where interest was allocated, this was usually through the introduction of new computerised accounting methods. Where costs had been incurred in introducing such accounting methods, the cost of doing so was often offset by increasing the management fee.

For most managing agents and landlords, however, the issue of paying interest was said to be irrelevant. A managing agent explains:

> *"Probably I should have put [the service charge money] into some form of interest paying account, which I haven't, I have just kept it fluid. And I've kept it fluid because I thought I was going to start the work ... I suppose they could turn round and say they're probably about thirty quid short 'cause it should have gone in an interest paying account."* (Managing agent/landlord, Brighton)

Most managing agents and landlords spoke about the 'fluid' nature of service charge accounts and felt that paying interest was almost an irrelevance. This was particularly so for large management operations with dozens of payments and cheques occurring each week. In such cases the money was kept on a current account for quick and easy access.

Many felt that the amount of interest likely to be earned was so little that it was not worth the added complication of shuffling money between current and interest bearing accounts. For others, this was a non-issue as they felt that there was rarely a surplus of cash on which to earn interest. Overall, most felt that guidelines would be helpful:

> *"I have transactions in and out every day of the week which makes it significantly different to a solicitor [who may also hold money in trust]. Plus, the Act gives no guidelines, like, well, if the balance is only 10% of the total year's expenditure you can keep that in a day-to-day account and not earn interest; it doesn't matter what the rules are. Give me some rules, we don't know."* (Managing agent, Paddington)

One suggestion that emerged was where there were sufficient monies available, a certain sum should be kept on an instant access current account to allow for the payment of regular bills. The remainder should be place on deposit in an interest bearing account. Another managing agent suggested that service charge accounts could be treated according to Law Society rules. This was his proposal, based on his understanding of the Law Society rules:

> *"If you hold a balance of a significant sum for more than seven days you must allow interest, if you have a balance for a much smaller sum you can have up to two months before you have to allow interest; fairly common sense, and it's a sliding scale, as the value goes down you can hold it for longer without giving interest."* (Managing agent, Paddington)

Tenants had generally little to say about the need for service charge payments to be held in interest bearing accounts; they were generally far more concerned about the quality of service and levels of management fees charged. Generally, most felt that the money should earn interest, but often recognised that this was not practical where the service charge money was quickly spent. However, there was some concern amongst those people who contributed to 'sinking funds' about the way the money was invested. For example, one leaseholder argued:

"It's not that [the money] has not been utilised properly, but that the sinking fund should have probably been invested better to get more interest back."
(Leaseholder, Manchester, Purpose-built block of flats)

Charging interest to service charge accounts

A final issue concerns what happens when the service charge accounts run into deficit. For many managing agents this was not a relevant issue saying that if sufficient funds were not available, the work would not be carried out, and services would not be provided until sufficient funds were forthcoming. This was not always the case, however. Some managing agents wanted the facility to 'overdraw' service charge accounts or borrow money to fund refurbishment. An issue that arises concerns how the interest can be recovered. A Paddington managing agent takes up the issue:

"They've (the Department of the Environment) brought in a statutory instrument to say these are the areas where you can put the money ... fairly tame which is as it should be ... but there's a whole lot of other rules that should be there, especially when overnight they've swept something into place that never existed. You see, they [the Department] come up with things about interest, alright, it's clear it means interest earned. What about when there's a deficit, who funds it, the trust fund? There should be a rule, it's all very well to say it depends on what the lease says, but the leases never contemplated a trust management." (Managing agent, Paddington)

4.5 Insurance of the property (Section 43)

Three main issues arose in connection with the property insurance; obtaining copies of the insurance documents, challenging the choice of insurance and making a claim. We review these in turn.

Obtaining the insurance documents

In many instances leaseholders had been provided with details of the building's insurance cover. However, where they had not been supplied, a few tenants had tried to obtain copies of the policy documents with varying degrees of success; in one instance a delay of 6 months occurred; two others were denied access; another was given an out of date policy; one tenant was charged for inspecting the policy. A number of respondents felt that some landlords and managing agents were very reluctant to provide the property insurance details;

"I tried to get the details [of the policy]. I wrote twice asking for details. We were assured that we did have insurance. I've never actually received a copy of any documents and I haven't got anything official. But they have assured us we are insured ... I was basically promised something through but I never did. You just get tired of asking." (Leaseholder, Paddington)

Some people were concerned about the building being under insured but were in a difficult position because the landlord refused to release any details. One tenant living in a converted flat was told that the building was not insured because the landlord had said it was too expensive to do so.

One difficulty that was raised by managing agents arose because of the use of 'group insurance'. Generally, managing agents said that they could obtain more competitive quotes by insuring all the properties managed under a single policy. Two issues arose. First, tenants often found the certificates issued less than reassuring as the insurance company rarely itemised the properties covered on the certificate. Second, managing agents were not always keen to release the insurance schedules because this showed all the properties they managed, which they felt was confidential information. This was by no means a major issue, but a dilemma which faced both managing agents and landlords. It partly accounts for the reluctance, by some managing agents, in releasing insurance documents.

In general, tenants felt that the provisions concerning property insurance in the 1987 Act were weak;

> *"It's like everything else in the Act. It hasn't got any teeth. Okay, so he [managing agent] doesn't comply, so what do we do, go to Court. Marvellous, more expense for us, which we probably won't get back, for something he [managing agent] is supposed to do in the first place. He should be fined and made to give it to us - court's no good, it's expensive, takes ages, and he's just as likely to comply just as we go to court and make us lose all our costs and legal expenses to teach us a lesson and make us less likely to go to court again. They do this you know ... I've seen it happen."*
> (Brighton Leaseholder, converted house; with experience of taking court action against a managing agent)

Challenging the choice of insurance

There had been little experience amongst this sample of people in challenging the landlord's choice of insurance company. One managing agent knew about two leaseholders living in a purpose-built block he managed who wished to change the of company. However, the company to be used was written in to their lease; they were unwilling to pursue a variation of the lease because of the potential costs involved.

One respondent had taken issue with the rise in premium that he was asked to pay and took the landlord to court using the 1987 legislation. The court found in his favour but only after considerable anguish and effort on his part:

> *"When the penthouse was built on the top of our block of flats, our insurance went up almost overnight by about 33%. I couldn't see any good reason for that, and it took me a long time to figure out what this criminal [landlord] was doing upstairs. He was offsetting the cost of insuring his penthouse onto us. Now it's one thing to think you're being defrauded, it's quite another to prove it and it took me many months of work to do it. We would not pay the increased premiums, and he said 'okay, there won't be any insurance. If you have a fire, you don't get a penny'. We paid what we thought was the right premium and no more, we went to the insurance company and we told them. They'd been forbidden to write to us, but we still went to see them, and the judge found in our favour, and we got damages and costs, but this takes months and months and months of work."* (Paddington, Leaseholder, on behalf of Residents association)

An issue that arose in one of the group discussions attended by leaseholders of purpose built blocks of flats in Croydon concerned insurance of the common parts of the building. Should this be covered by the building's insurance, usually arranged by the landlord or managing agent, or by the tenants' contents insurance? The tenants were told that the building's insurance only covered the exterior of the building. The interior, including the common parts should be covered by the tenants individual contents' insurance policies. The issue was felt to be a 'grey area' and remained unresolved.

Making an insurance claim

Most of the landlords and their agents were aware that tenants had a right to notify insurance companies of a claim; tenants were less aware of their rights made under the 1987 Act. Generally, this provision was viewed as 'fair' although it was often pointed out that it was common courtesy to notify the managing agent or landlord first. Where the policy number was withheld from tenants, which was often the case, then notification direct to the insurance company was usually impossible. There were often other complications too. A solicitor identified these problems:

> *"Let's put it this way, the whole question of insurance needs looking at ... it's not clear what 'noting' means legally and it's not at all clear what it means, for example, if you've got policies in your joint names and insurance companies make the cheques out to you jointly. Getting the money back from the landlord can be a helluva business. I've had more than half a dozen cases over the past couple of years where they have made claims and then the landlord(s) won't pay the money over - oh, we'll set it off against the service charges, they never do."* (Solicitor)

A small number of tenants had shared the same experience. In all cases they were still awaiting payment; in one case the leaseholder had been trying to be reimbursed for 18 months.

A solution to this problem is offered by the same solicitor:

> *"Any tenant who can show that he's been making the payments should be entitled to make the claim direct and have it settled direct and have it paid to him direct, subject to the insurance company being satisfied there's no fraud or anything like that."*

4.6 The role of tenants'/residents' associations (Section 41, Schedule 2)

A number of issues were raised about the provisions relating to Tenants' Associations. These related to three areas of concern: recognition of tenants' associations, their rights, and the operation of 'consultation' in practice.

Recognition of Tenants' Associations (TAs)

Many tenants were not aware of the process by which associations could become recognised although most thought that access to such information would be relatively easy to come by through one of the many advisory organisations that operate locally. Questions were often raised as to the guidelines that regulate the recognition of TAs. A number of people had been challenged about their TAs operation and constitution and said that managing agents would sometimes use this as a way of avoiding consultation. One managing agent summed up the opinion of many of the tenants and other managing agents:

> *"There needs to be formal guidelines for the constitution of a TA. Why should two out of a block of a hundred form a TA and be recognised... there needs to be formal guidelines that regulates the recognition of TAs..... currently, the Rent Assessment Panel, which tenants can use to gain recognition, uses **informal** guidelines."* (Our emphasis)

The rights of TAs

Conflicting views arose about the rights of TAs. This was primarily in connection with the right to consultation over building work. As leaseholders and a number of managing agents argued, why should TAs receive more information, such as detailed building specifications, than tenants when it is the tenants who are paying? By contrast, another managing agent could not see why this provision had been included in the 1987 Act as it duplicated, in his view, an existing right:

"Under the 1985 Landlord and Tenant Act everyone is consulted anyway - copies of specifications have to be displayed and copies of estimates attached to Section 20 notices and circulated to all tenants, so what does this [Act] do that is so new?" (Managing agent)

Consultation with TAs

Tenants' Associations have the right to be consulted in certain circumstances. The provision of the right to consult was seen as fairly ineffectual in connection with both building works and the appointment of a managing agent. For example, one leaseholder summed up the views of many others:

"It still seems a flimsy way of going about it because even if you (TA) are recognised, all you can make is an observation; which doesn't hold up in a court of law. If the landlord is going to go and do it, he will." (Leaseholder)

"The right to consult isn't really worth anything. If we did consult and if the landlord wrote and said we're appointing Blaggs & Co. as managing agents and we wrote back and said we don't want Blaggs & Co, we want Bill Smith, or someone, the landlord can just write back and say thank you very much, we've consulted you, we're still going to appoint Blaggs & Co. Simple as that." (Leaseholder, Paddington)

4.7 Variation of leases (Part IV)

Of all the tenants interviewed two had used Part IV of the 1987 Act, a further three had considered doing so. The two people who had applied for a variation of their lease had done so on the grounds that the division of the individual service charge bills, when summed, came to more than 100% of the total demand. Their application was successful and the process was found to be relatively easy. However, the cost was thought to be unacceptable for a relatively simple amendment to the lease. The cost totalled £3,000, shared amongst eight people.

Those leaseholders who had considered a deed of variation had done so for different reasons. In one case, this was to allow for a six monthly, rather than an annual collection of service charges. In another, each flat was responsible for their own portion of the building's insurance, which meant that there was no guarantee that the whole building was insured. A deed of variation was proposed to rectify this. A third example concerned the establishment of a sinking fund, which was not currently written into the lease. In each case, the leaseholders had decided not to proceed with a variation of the lease on grounds of cost.

"It's a very protracted and difficult job and it has to go before the court ... can you imagine the cost?" (Leaseholder, Manchester)

"We just have [an informal] agrement with the managing agent to pay half yearly ... we did enquire about doing that [variation of lease] but it involved quite a bit of expense ... so again it's legal costs." (Leaseholder, Brighton)

While this Part of the Act was generally seen as a "good piece of legislation", there were four points of procedure that were raised.

First, while the legislative procedures required to vary a lease were seen as fairly simple, the mechanics, and therefore cost, of doing so can be prohibitive. For example, up to seven parties can be involved in agreeing the deed of variation: the lessees, the lessees' solicitor(s), the managing agent, the freeholder and their solicitors, and the mortgage company(ies), and their solicitors. One landlord had experience of being involved in varying a lease. He takes up the story:

> *"It actually resulted from the fact that the lessees wanted us to do something with the service charge reserve fund which couldn't be done under the terms of the lease and we were willing to do it so long as they got the consent of every single person who had contributed to that fund. And they couldn't achieve it, so they then took the case to court to see if they could get the court to amend the lease to allow this to be done. The court said, 'Well you've got to go and get all the consents from all the original lessees', and it has honestly been going on for two or three years ... partly because some people are being difficult, but others are abroad and can't be traced."*

In the same context, one tenant who had used this provision felt that *"getting 75% to consent and no more than 10% oppose is a stupendous undertaking"*. He felt that a *"simple majority"* would be fairer.

Second, a number of people thought that the provision was *"terribly restrictive as to the circumstances in which it applies"*:

> *"These powers, although useful, seem unlikely to be widely used, especially as an application to vary a lease may be made on only one or more of the grounds specified in Section 35"* (Leaseholder, Brighton)

In this context respondents felt that two additional issues should be specifically included in this Part of the Act. First, where landlords retain a flat in the building for their own use, it is not unknown for the landlords share of the service charge to be distributed across the other leaseholders in the building. Second, a similar practice can occur where there are rented flats in the block - their maintenance is included within the leaseholders service charge payments. Explicit facilities to correct these practices were recommended by a small number of tenants and advisors alike.

Third, an element of unfairness was identified in the Act as it currently stands:

> *"if the service charge percentages add up to more than 100%, that's one of the grounds for an application to have the lease varied. But if they don't add up to 100%, and that happens because solicitors make a mistake on conveyancing or somebody drops the wrong figure in a lease, there's no right [of redress]. ..... if a landlord gets back £90 for every £100 he spends you're going to restrict the number of hundreds you spend."* (Managing agent)

Fourth, in some cases, it is possible for a tenant to lose out through a variation in their lease. For example, if they have a low service charge, and a variation of the lease is approved by court that increases their service charge contribution, this could penalise them. It was pointed out that where leases are varied, although it may be to the benefit of the majority, there may be a minority who are penalised. They should, it was argued, be entitled to compensation. The question arises as to who pays for the compensation - the landlord, the managing agent, the service charge account, those who voted for the variation of the lease, or some other compensatory body.

Whilst discussing the issue of variation of leases there was considerable discussion about the format and content of leases. This will be separately discussed in Chapter 6.

4.8 Appointment of a manager by the court (Part II)

Two tenants living in the same block of flats had used the powers granted under Sections 21 to 24 of the 1987 Act to have a manager appointed by the court. The circumstances have already been referred to in which one million pounds worth of refurbishment work were carried out, but to an inferior standard. In addition, the tenants had numerous problems with the landlord and managing agent over disputed service charges, including a service account that was *"adrift by about £5,000"*. They decided that the only way to gain control of the maintenance of the building was to acquire the freehold themselves; seeking the appointment of a manager was a first step in this process:

> *"This was when the building was collapsing into the street practically, with large chunks of masonry coming down ... it's one of the essential steps that you take towards getting hold of the freehold. You're proving to the court that he is not doing his job, that he's incompetent, or whatever. And this must strengthen your case when you eventually go to court to get the freehold ... by proving negligence .. you need this history."*

While the legal action was successful, it was not without its difficulties:

> *"Getting damages is another matter. This is another deterrent to civil, not criminal, [cases]. When you serve summonses on the landlord you put what they call a penal clause on it and if he doesn't comply he goes to prison ... but we had the business of employing bailiffs and all that kind of thing to distrain his property, and get his car, and see if we could get that towed away and sold at auction ... in fact the only way we found that we could really move him was a bankruptcy petition, and then he paid."*

One other tenant, living in a Paddington mansion block, who also had "nightmare experiences" with the management of the block considered legal action under part II of the Act but did not proceed because:

> *"we have not the money or the strength left to do that."*

Although these were the only circumstances in which the appointment of a manager had been considered by this sample of respondents there were numerous criticisms of this part of the legislation. Some respondents felt that this provision was fundamentally flawed; others considered the principle to be correct but felt that the procedures by which the appointment of a manager was accomplished to be problematic. First we consider the reasons why some respondents felt this provision was flawed.

Perceived flaws in Part II of the 1987 Act

While it was recognised that Part II of the Act was intended to apply only in extreme circumstances of poor management, a number of people felt that this intention itself was the fundamental flaw in the legislation. This was because the legislation only came into play when management issues had reached a serious state. As one leaseholder argued:

> *"This is intended for serious and continuing breaches of the landlords/managing agents obligations. Surely there should be something that happens, or could happen well before problems got to such a serious level."* (Leaseholder, Paddington Mansion block)

In this instance, the existing remedies in the 1987 Act were not thought to be sufficient to meet this need.

Another leaseholder felt that this Part of the Act was flawed for a different set of reasons which were related to the ability of people to be able to afford the cost of legal action:

"The provision is fundamentally flawed ..... people owning a £100,000 flat aren't going to let them get into this state of disrepair ... people who buy flats that are already in a bad state are going to be poorer - they wouldn't have bought them in the first place otherwise - and they aren't going to be able to afford the cost of legal action [to pursue the appointment of a manager]."

One Croydon landlord felt that if problems had reached such a level, then the right to apply to the courts for an appointment of a manager was insufficient remedy. He explains:

"If it gets this bad, shouldn't the problem be solved by automatically giving the leaseholders the opportunity to buy the freehold ... the thought of going through 'appointment of a manager' and 'compulsory acquisition' ... takes at least five years and I can't think about how much money .... seems totally inappropriate. Let them [leaseholders] have an automatic right to make an offer for the freehold in cases like this." (Landlord, Croydon)

One Paddington leaseholder, discussing the problems that Tenants' Associations had had with their managing agent felt that the provision only addressed problems in which little, or no maintenance was being carried out. However, in their block, the agents were, it was felt, commissioning excessive works in order to reap the benefits of an increased management fee. Counsel had advised them that Part II did not apply in such cases, an omission they felt seriously undermined the intentions of the legislation.

Procedural difficulties

Turning now to the procedural aspects of the appointment of a manager a number of difficulties with the provision emerged. Some of these difficulties arise from the way in which the provision has been drafted, others concern what were seen as omissions or inconsistencies with this piece of legislation. There was also a feeling that the provision was open to abuse by unscrupulous landlords.

Issues arising from the drafting of Part II

In terms of the way in which the provision has been drafted, there are four main issues that arise. First, some respondents, primarily managing agents, felt that the process was far too lengthy requiring the need to serve notice, delays in getting to court, and the time required for the landlord to take remedial action. A much simpler and more elegant solution, it was argued, would be to use a panel of independent surveyors to assess the degree to which the property was being adequately maintained with a local ombudsman to adjudicate. This, it was felt, would provide for a swifter and substantially less expensive way of determining whether a manager should be appointed.

Second, where disputes arose about the quality of management, at present, the onus was said to be on the tenants to prove that the property management had been poor. A number of respondents felt that this should be reversed and that as managing agents and landlords are providing a service it should be for them to demonstrate that the management had been satisfactory. This brings us to the third issue. In order to show that the building has been badly managed considerable expense would be incurred, tenants said, as they would have to obtain professional advice and opinion. The question arises as to how this should be paid for. Tenants generally argued that it was the landlord and/or the managing agent who should be liable.

After all, it was pointed out, managing agents are contracted to the landlords to carry out a service, not to the tenants.

Fourth, the drafting of this section was felt to have left a 'grey area' in need of definition. For example, landlords are required to take remedial action in a 'reasonable' time; a number of tenants felt that this length of time should be specified in the Act as it provided a potentially easy way for landlords, or their agents, to *"take their time in putting things right, if ever"*.

Inconsistencies and omissions

This part of the legislation was felt to be inconsistent with the rest of the Act and arises out of the requirement that only one lessee needs to take action and serve notice on the landlord. However, as one managing agent argued;

> *"if it's that bad I would imagine you will find there should be more than one tenant who thinks that. To set such a low threshold of one seems totally unfair. Other areas [of the Act] they've talked about majorities. I would have thought to be fair you should be talking about half the tenants [before one can proceed]."*

Three omissions were also specified. First, it was pointed out by a small number of housing advisors that in cases where action is being taken under Part II of the Act, the building will continue to deteriorate. Not all maintenance costs are recoverable from the leaseholders, it depends on the terms of their leases. Additionally, some of the remedial work may have arisen because of the landlords' disinterest in the fabric of the building. Consequently, leaseholders may not necessarily be liable to pay for the full cost of the repairs. In such cases, provision for borrowing was thought to be essential. It was suggested that:

> *"there should be an explicit provision included [in the Act] to say that the [appointed] managing agent can borrow on behalf of the landlord and recover that money from the landlord, if necessary by registering a charge on their property, their personal property so that they can spend money on the repairs that they may have to do under the terms of the court order without incurring personal liability for that."*

Second, a small number of managing agents felt that they should have a statutory 'right of reply' in the process of appointing a manager.

Third, a small number of respondents, primarily managing agents, pointed out that if this Part of the Act were to be implemented then a receiver manager was not necessarily the most appropriate person to be appointed to manage a property - *"what do they know about property management, their expertise is finance and insolvency, not property management"*. One of the managing agents mentioned a recently reported case in which a residents' association had been appointed by the court to act as manager. This was thought to be both an innovative use of the provision and a potentially beneficial remedy to the tenants problems. Guidelines, however, had been omitted from the Act; it was felt, by these respondents, to be essential to provide such advice in order that the person(s) appointed by the court was able to manage the property in a professional and satisfactory manner.

Evading the provisions of the Act

A number of leaseholders felt that procedurally this provision was likely to be foiled by the actions of the landlord. For example:

"An unscrupulous landlord can, however, by remedying some of the breaches, but doing nothing about others place the tenants in a dilemma whether to proceed with the application to the court having regard to the expense and to the uncertainty of the outcome or whether to give the landlord further time to remedy the outstanding breaches. The opportunity is wide open to the landlord to use delaying tactics to frustrate the tenants."
(Leaseholder, Brighton)

A small number of leaseholders in Croydon and Paddington had known instances where a scenario such as this had occurred. Court action had been started, incurring considerable legal costs and at the point of the court hearing the landlords took some remedial action; the tenants were at a loss to know whether to proceed or to drop the case. Either way, their ability to recoup all of their legal costs was in doubt. The tenants in this instance dropped the case and the landlord ceased the remedial work. As one tenant commented: *"A landlord may promise in court to put things right but may not do so. This then requires another court action, at considerable expense and with further delay."*

Overview

Although the spirit of this provision was generally viewed as *"just and right"* by the majority of respondents, the necessity for court action, the need for expert witnesses, the potential expense and the delays likely to be incurred were thought to considerably weaken the effectiveness of Part II of the Act as a solution to management problems. Most people, when asked, expressed considerable doubt about whether they would be prepared to use this provision. In general, they felt that if conditions had become this bad, they would prefer to sell their flat and leave the problem behind them.

4.9 Compulsory acquisition of the property (Part III)

None of the respondents interviewed had direct experience of the compulsory acquisition of a property. A solicitor, however, who had been involved in the appointment of a receiver/manager for a block of flats which had serious problems had been instructed to proceed under Part III of the Act and was waiting for the expiry of the three year time period imposed by the legislation. The property was described as *"falling to pieces ... there were subsidence claims outstanding ... the tenants couldn't get insurance because of fraud claims"*. He did not envisage any problems:

> *"I imagine the court will make the order because the landlord's made no attempt to try and get the order lifted and produce his own decent managing agent."*

Overall, the majority of respondents felt that this was an acceptable right, but to be used only 'in extremis'. However, there were two objections to the principle of this part of the Act. Both were of a fundamental nature and raised by managing agents and landlords. First, some felt that this was an unnecessary piece of legislation as the remedy already existed under Part II of the 1987 Act. Second, some people felt that compulsory acquisition was not a right that an individual citizen should have;

> *"I am wholly opposed to anything of that nature. I do not believe that one man should be given the right to acquire another man's property. That's something that in my view should only be done by the state. [For example] if it needs a property, or something like that, for state purposes, like road building, hospital building or something of that nature. I do not believe one*

individual should be given the right to acquire another man's property."
(Landlord, Paddington)

Five main issues were raised in relation to the potential usability of the right to compulsorily acquire the freeholder's interest in a property. First, tenants, in particular, felt that the requirement for a **collective** purchase was burdensome. In some cases, it was pointed out that people simply did not want to buy, in others people could not afford to buy. Although it was recognised that a nominated organisation such as a housing association could purchase the property, or individual flats within the property, overall, the need for a collective purchase was considered unnecessarily bureaucratic. A number of respondents felt that instead of being required to collectively purchase the property each individual should have the right to purchase or nominate a purchaser themselves.

Second, considerable discussion focused on how the building should be valued for sale. Section 31 provides for the terms of the disposal to be determined by the rent assessment committee. Under Section 31 (2) the value of the landlord's interest is determined as:

'an amount equal to the amount which, in their opinion, that interest might be expected to realise if sold on the open market by a willing seller on the appropriate terms and on the assumption that none of the tenants of the landlord of any premises comprised in those premises was buying or seeking to buy that interest'.

For example:

> *"if you went to court and they said 'yes you have the right to buy', its strictly market value [Section 31 (2)]. But [the court] ignores the tenants' bids. The valuation assumption is ignoring the tenants' bids. Now in any leasehold or freehold situation it is the tenants that are key to it ... when you value the building you must also take into account the tenants' interest [as leaseholders] and look at that value otherwise you wouldn't be advising the freeholder correctly. Tenants' bid are always significant in a leasehold situation, so it is unfair that they should be ignored in the valuation."*
> (Managing agent, Paddington)

Third, it was felt that there was a potential 'grey area' in this provision as landlords are required to be given a 'reasonable' period of time in which to remedy the complaint. However, there are no guidelines as to how the length of a reasonable period of time is to be determined thereby providing an opportunity for intransigent landlords to use delaying tactics.

Fourth, there was a general feeling that the requirement for there to have been a management order under Part II of the Act in operation for the previous three years was unnecessarily lengthy. For example:

> *"... it is totally ridiculous for a managing agent to continue like this for three years ... I would have resigned well before this ... it should happen much earlier if there is no intention to manage the property ... a year is enough ... six months notice to do the works and a further six months to complete"*
> (Managing agent, Croydon)

> *"Three years! You've probably moved on by then.. that's no good."*
> (Leaseholder, Brighton, converted flat)

Finally, the cost of court action was raised a number of times in the context of discussing the provision of compulsory acquisition:

> *"You can't force your freeholder to sell without spending an awful lot of money on the legal process... I can't see it being very easy to bring about a change in landlords, or agents, without enormous expense".* (Managing agent, Brighton)

Two specific issues regarding legal costs were mentioned. First, for most legal actions of this sort, considerable amounts of money are required at the start of the action; it was generally felt that few people would have access to sufficient amounts of money to be able to proceed. Second, even if one did proceed and win the case, it was mentioned a number of times that there was no guarantee of recouping all of the costs incurred. This was considered to be one of the main factors prohibiting legal action under Part III of the 1987 Act. We continue with a discussion of the issue of legal costs and court action in Chapter 6.

4.10 Right of first refusal (Part I)

Eleven respondents interviewed had been offered the freehold under Section 5 of the Act; 8 were successful. In a further five cases, the rights under Part I of the Act had not been conferred. In each case the tenants had attempted to force a sale under section 12 of the Act (the right of qualifying tenants to compel a sale by the new landlord). Of these five instances, one resulted in a successful purchase.

It was the view of a number of the advisors interviewed that Part I of the Act was widely disregarded by landlords:

> *"We look in the auction catalogues and then let the tenants know ... landlords frequently ignore section 5 ... it's too much hassle for them, they just ignore the tenants and ignore the law."* (Local authority advisor)

Landlords and managing agents confirmed this view; some also admitted to the disposal of freeholds without first offering them to the tenants.

In this section we review people's experiences of buying the freehold, either where the right of first refusal has been conferred, or where tenants have forced a sale. We continue with a discussion of the logistics of buying a freehold under Part I of the Act and consider some of the difficulties that the legislation presents.

Buying the freehold - where the right of first refusal had been conferred

We turn now to people's experiences of purchasing the freeholds. In the majority of cases where the right of first refusal was conferred, the tenants eventually bought the property. Almost all of those who had been involved in the purchase of the freehold recounted how difficult it was to collectively raise sufficient money to purchase the block, it was difficult to meet the statutory deadlines, and the venture was stressful and time consuming. These issues will be explored in more detail later in the chapter.

In a couple of instances tenants agreed that they were not interested in pursuing the purchase and allowed the offer to lapse. In other instances, while some had been keen to pursue the landlord's offer, insufficient interest amongst all the tenants meant that the purchase of the property was not pursued.

Two issues arise from this. First, while collective purchase may be an acceptable principle, the lack of interest of some of the residents living in the block effectually penalises those who do want to buy the freehold to their flat.

E

Second, where a situation such as this arises it is possible to nominate another individual, company or housing association to buy either the complete block, or a collection of individual flats. In practice, however, this was found to be very difficult to accomplish. In part this was because of a declining property market - few companies were prepared to purchase in a falling market. However, respondents also said that investment companies tended only to be interested where there were a substantial number of leases for sale. For example, in a block of 150 units in which, say 50, were for sale, companies were likely to be interested. However, far less interest was thought to be generated over the potential sale of two flats in a block comprising eight units. We did encounter two situations in which an investment company had been involved. For example, in one block of 167 flats of which 50 were rented, an investment company bought the leases to the rented flats while a resident-owned property company bought the leases to the remaining flats. Nevertheless, for many people the condition of collective purchase was felt to be restrictive.

However, the difficulty of collective negotiation had not arisen where the freehold was purchased by a registered housing association. In this instance, the association negotiated for the purchase of the freehold and then made individual arrangements with each of the tenants.

A further example of tenants turning down an offer to buy the freehold arises because of the condition attached to the sale by the landlord. Against a background of *"appalling management"*, and a history of considerable cost over-runs, poor quality workmanship, charging for services that were not provided, and disputed service charge accounts, the landlord offered the tenants the opportunity to buy the freehold. However, the offer was made subject to the tenants retaining the existing managing agents, in perpetuity. Because of this history and the suspicion that the landlord and the managing agent were one and the same, the tenants felt obliged to reject the offer. They did not seek advice as to the legality of the condition imposed.

Buying the freehold - where the right of first refusal had NOT been conferred

In the course of the study we encountered five instances where tenants were aware that the freehold of the property was about to change hands without the right of first refusal being conferred. None of these disposals were exempted under section 4 of the 1987 Act. A number of other tenants thought that the landlord had changed since commencement of the Act but did not have sufficient information to prove that this was the case.

Of the five instances where the landlord had not complied with the Act, two had become aware of this *"too late"* had and not taken any further action. One had their counter offer rejected and the landlord subsequently sold to another party. In this instance the property was felt to have been offered at a price substantially above market value. Another tenant recounted how they had abandoned the sale because between the time of the offer and the date set for exchange of contracts, house prices had fallen such that the property became 'over-priced'. The remaining tenant had been involved in a collective negotiation for the property in which a registered housing association had been nominated as the purchaser. The purchase was successful.

All of this group of people identified the same difficulties with the process of purchasing a freehold under Part I of the 1987 Act mentioned earlier. Difficulties with collectively raising sufficient finance to purchase the block, meeting the statutory deadlines, and the stressful and time consuming nature of such a venture were all mentioned. Again, individual rather than collective purchase of individual flats was felt to be preferential and considered to be a potential solution to the difficulties mentioned.

The issue of selling a property without informing the tenants was often contentious. A number of people felt that despite the legal redress already available under sections 15 and 16, the Act did not go far enough in penalising landlords for non-compliance. As a number of people argued, in order to compel a sale to the tenants recourse to court action is necessary. This involves people in a great deal of expense. This usually has to be provided at the beginning of any proceedings, and there is no guarantee of recouping all their expenditure.

Some people, primarily tenants and advisors, felt that Part I (Right of first refusal) should include a financial penalty, others thought that the freehold should automatically revert to the tenants, collectively, without recourse to the court. Landlords, however, were generally opposed to such suggestions.

An issue that arose in this context concerned the responsibility of managing agents in informing tenants of a change of freeholder. They were divided over this. On the one hand, some felt that as their contract was with the landlord, their responsibilities and obligations were only to carry out the landlord's wishes. Others, however, felt that despite their contractual obligations to the landlord they were morally, though not necessarily legally, obliged to inform tenants when the landlord intended to side-step the law.

Managing agents were roughly equally divided over whether they would enter into the management of a property in which the right of first refusal had not been offered. The reasons for this were two-fold. Those who would manage such a property said that there was no illegality in doing so as the tenants still had rights under the Act to purchase the freehold. Others, however, while agreeing that such a transaction was not illegal felt that it *"said something about the landlord and the managing agent"*. They felt that this reflected on the managing agent and could potentially sour the tenant-managing agent relationship from the outset. This, they felt, was not good business practice.

Although not mentioned very often, there was a strength of feeling amongst leaseholders that managing agents should be required, by statute, to inform them when the landlord intended to dispose of the freehold.

The logistics of buying the freehold

The scale of properties involved in this study varied considerably from a converted house containing 8 units to a mansion block containing 167 units. Despite this, people's experiences of buying the freehold under section 5 of the 1987 Act tended to be very similar. Almost without exception, tenants felt that the purchase of the freehold had been worthwhile. However, they commented strongly on the way the legislation had been drafted. There were three emergent themes: difficulties with finding out about the process of buying a freehold under the 1987 Act; the time periods specified by the provision; and valuation. In addition, two 'grey areas' emerged that were thought to be in need of clarification.

Information about how to buy the freehold

In almost all cases, respondents found the letter sent to them conferring the right of first refusal to be terse and uninformative. In some cases people thought it was *"almost a joke"* and put it to one side:

> *"Well, I got this letter saying that if I could raise 1.3 million pounds I could buy the property. I mean, what would you do with a letter like that ... it was*

only when [another tenant] called a meeting, she's a solicitor, that it began to seem possible." (Brighton, Leaseholder; offer lapsed as sufficient finance could not be raised)

Many thought that the initial offer should be much more informative and should lay out the procedure and timings required under the legislation. They also felt that this should be a statutory obligation.

As an example of 'good practice' one organisation was said to be extremely helpful. With a policy of encouraging tenants to buy the freehold, their letter containing the offer included a summary of the procedures required; the relevant Department of the Environment information booklet was also enclosed. This was viewed very favourably by tenants.

Comments about the specified periods	In most cases tenants felt that the time periods specified in this Part of the Act were too short; this was particularly so where the block comprised a large number of units. Co-ordinating large numbers of tenants, arranging valuations, arranging finance - *"you can't just go into your bank manager and say 'can I have 1.5 million pounds?' you know"* - and meeting the time scales laid down in the Act was said to be a very difficult task:

> *"I did sweat blood. Probably for four or five months I was in meetings four nights a week [arranging the purchase]. A lot of those meetings were going from eight at night till four in the morning ... I wouldn't do it again, but if I am in a situation in a block where it comes up for offer, yes, I would make sure it is done."* (Paddington, Leaseholder; mansion block comprising 167 units)

Many mentioned that they *"only just"* met the deadlines. In one instance, it was only through the generosity of the landlord in extending the time that the purchase was able to be completed.

By contrast, landlords and managing agents felt that the time periods were too long as they effectively 'locked' the landlord into a price it could be a disadvantage. While this could be advantageous to the landlord in a falling market, in times of rising house prices it could be a disadvantage. In addition, there was the view that sometimes landlords needed a 'quick sale', perhaps to aid the company's cash flow, which was now prohibited by Part I of the 1987 Act. Tenants, too, recognised that by fixing the sale price there were both benefits and disadvantages. The only suggestion received in resolution of this problem centred on the requirement to collectively negotiate; many respondents suggested that the right to individually purchase the freehold to a flat would alleviate these problems to a considerable extent and reduce the time scale in which the purchase could be completed.

An issue raised by one tenant in relation to the time consuming nature of collective negotiation concerned the tracing of lessees where flats had been sub-let. This was described as a *"nightmare task"* within the time scales permitted. However, this respondent could not see any acceptable solution other than that already suggested - the need for individual rather than collective negotiation and purchase of freeholds.

Property valuation	The third major theme to emerge concerned the valuation of the property prior to purchase. Some people commissioned a surveyor to value the property. Others argued that the condition of the property was not material to the offer price and

negotiated on the basis of the local property prices and what they felt they could afford to offer. Nevertheless the issue of valuation was problematic.

In most cases, the tenants had paid the asking price. In two instances, the tenants had made a counter bid. In one instance the landlord sold to another party; in the other the landlord made a counter-counter-bid. This was accepted.

Some respondents suggested the price paid should be the *"market value"* of the vacant property; others felt that the price should reflect that it comprised 'sitting tenants'. Managing agents and landlords, in particular, pointed out that the land may have a development value in excess of the value of the building. Which, it was asked, should the landlord be able to select? The Act, it was thought, was silent on these points and in need of clarification.

'Grey areas'

Three aspects of this provision were felt to be in need of clarification. The first concerns the issue of how the legislation should operate in cases where there are flats above business premises. As it stands, the Act does not apply when more than 50% of the property is used for purposes other than residential use. However, as one managing agent pointed out the use of floor space as a deciding factor has no commercial basis. Take, for example, the case where the flats above a shop may occupy considerably more than 50% of the floor space (excluding common parts) yet represents considerably less than 50% of the value of the property. If the landlord wishes to sell the freehold, despite the fact that the flats may represent, say, only 10% of the value of the property, the Act still applies. This was an issue that arose only once. However, it was felt that the intention of the Act had become muddled at this point and was in need of clarification.

The issue of 'common parts' and their definition was raised on a separate occasion. The usual assumption is that common parts relate to stairs, hallways, entrance ways, etc. However, if a landlord wished to sell a lease for a roof development, one managing agent queried whether roofs were construed as a 'common part' of the building or whether it formed part of the flat(s) immediately underneath. His view was that the landlord retained rights over the development of the roof space - if he did not then this was seen as an unfair restriction on the landlord's ability to operate as a business. Nevertheless, this was felt to be a grey area in the Act and also in need of clarification.

Finally, an issue that arose in the context of the right of first refusal and concerned the extension of head leases. The managing agent takes up the story:

> *"I manage an estate ... where there are a lot of family leases on long leases but some of them are converted into flats... they're all held from the trustees on a head lease. The head lessee then grants sub-leases to the individual lessees. I cannot now extend the lease, the head lease, because before I do that the head lessee has to offer his lease to the residents before he can surrender it to the trustees so that they can grant him a longer lease. So it [the 1987 Act] causes a lot of problems really in that we can't deal with the head lease as easily as we could before."* (Managing agent, Paddington)

4.11 Overview

Throughout this chapter we have discussed respondents' experiences of using the provisions of the Landlord and Tenant Act 1987. Whilst the principle of the legislation was warmly welcomed, there was an overwhelming view that the effectiveness of the Act was impaired. In part this was felt to be because the legislation was over-complex and difficult to interpret. Procedural omissions and the lack of penalties and legal redress for non-compliance or the evasion of duties under the Act were also felt to be major limitations.

In the next chapter we discuss the 'tricks' which landlords and managing agents are said to use to circumvent or impair further the effectiveness of the legislation; a small number of 'loopholes' in the 1987 Act are also identified.

Chapter 5

The Effectiveness of the Landlord and Tenant Act 1987

Throughout the study it was apparent that when they became familiar with the terms of the 1987 Act, most people viewed the principle of the legislation in a favourable light. They felt that it provided tenants with useful rights whilst maintaining a reasonably equitable balance between the interests of leaseholders and their landlords. Nevertheless, there were some dissenting views: some felt that the balance has been tipped unfavourably against the landlord, an issue that was raised mostly in connection with the right of first refusal and compulsory acquisition of a landlord's interest. Others felt that by making Parts II, III and IV (Appointment of managers, Compulsory acquisition, and Variation of lease, respectively) apply only in extreme circumstances, the legislation provides little to stop landlord-tenant problems from escalating. In terms of the procedures laid down by the Act, and based on their experiences of using the legislation, many respondents felt that the Act was deficient in a number of areas.

The effectiveness with which a piece of legislation deals with relevant problems may be determined by two main factors - those that are related to the Act itself, and others which are extraneous to the Act but impinge on the process of using the legislation. In this chapter we focus on those factors that are related to the Act. In the next chapter (Chapter 6) attention is turned towards extraneous factors, in particular people's experiences of taking court action and their need for information about legislation relevant to their housing problems.

In considering the 1987 Act itself respondents raised a number of issues that were felt to limit the Act's effectiveness. These fell into one of four categories: features that were considered to have been omitted or procedures that were considered to be inadequate or cumbersome; features that were considered to be open to interpretation and in need of clarification ('grey areas'); methods which unscrupulous managing agents and landlords use to either circumvent the law, or reduce its effectiveness ('sharp practices'); and omissions or 'loopholes' within the Act that allow a landlord to escape from their legal duty.

5.1 Procedures

A number of procedural difficulties have been identified. In addition, there are a number of provisions which respondents felt would enhance the effectiveness of the 1987 Act but are currently omitted. In the majority of cases these difficulties relate to the lack of enforcement provision within the 1987 Act. Many tenants and advisors felt that the Act was "worthless" in practice because some of the provisions were unforceable. For example, there is no legal obligation for a landlord to reply to tenants' communications; unscrupulous managing agents and landlords can easily evade 'consultations' and ignore tenants' 'observations' without any legal redress.

Most concerns were expressed in relation to the service charge provisions. The need for statutory guidelines over consultations, and the strengthening of tenants' abilities to challenge service charges and excessive work frequently emerged. In this context, many tenants also felt that provisions to deal with disputes about the quality of services and building works were sadly lacking and considerably weakened this part of the legislation.

Table 5.1   Procedural deficiencies and omissions

Information about the landlord
Easy to evade by giving false name/address
Ineffective if landlord gives an accommodation address, box number, overseas address for contact, or refuses to reply
Need for financial penalty in instances of non-compliance

Service charges
Consultation' insufficiently defined
No legal redress under the 1987 Act where 'too much work' is carried out
The ability to challenge service charges considered to be ineffectual
Need for a provision whereby service charge monies can be withheld where services are not provided, or are of poor quality, or not functioning, without risk of forfeiture of lease
Need for ability to charge interest to service charge accounts when 'overdrawn'

Consultation over building works
'Observation' insufficiently defined; need for landlords/managing agents to provide written reasons for rejecting tenants estimates
Consultation time limits need to be specified
Approval of estimates by tenants - what percentage of tenants should approve estimates before work is carried out?
Lack of arbitration facilities in cases of dispute over building work estimates and specifications
Consultation limits easy to evade by tendering for a number of discrete pieces of work that fall beneath the statutory limit
No redress under the 1987 Act for poor quality work, after it has been carried out

Insurance of the property
The ability to 'challenge' the landlord's choice considered to be ineffective
Tenants to be legally entitled to receive insurance claim money direct
Financial penalties to be available where landlords refuse to supply copies of the insurance documents

Tenants associations (TA)
Need for formal guidelines concerning constitution, composition of TAs, and methods of recognition

Variation of leases
The range of conditions under which a deed of variation can be applied for considered to be too restrictive (eg inability to change a lease where the sum of individual payments add up to less than 100% of the total service charge demand)
Where a variation of a lease effectively penalises a leaseholder the Act is silent concerning the issue of compensation

Appointment of a manager by the court
Provision only applicable where too little work/services are provided, not where too much is provided
Determining whether the landlord/managing agent is carrying out their legal duties - how is this decided; who pays?
'Reasonable' time to take remedial action not defined
Need for statutory 'right of reply' for managing agent
Requires only one qualifying tenant to take action - felt to be too low a threshold and should be raised (e.g. 50% of qualifying tenants)
Procedures cumbersome, lengthy and costly

Compulsory acquisition
'Reasonable' time to take remedial action not defined
Method of property valuation to be defined
Procedures lengthy and costly - requirement that management order to have been operative for three years felt to be excessive

Right of first refusal
Time periods too long - penalises landlord
Time periods too short for tenants to arrange necessary finance, etc., especially where the block comprises a large number of flats
Need for individual rather than collective purchase of freehold - i.e. an individual should be able to buy the freehold to a single flat
Valuation problematic   1) market or development price?
                        2) where flats are located above shops
Need for financial penalty for not conferring right of first refusal (need to penalise for evasion/attempted evasion of the law)

Throughout the 1987 Act a range of procedural difficulties and omissions were identified by all parties concerned. These have been discussed fully in Chapters 3 and 4, and are summarised here in Table 5.1

5.2 'Grey areas'

A number of aspects of the 1987 Act were felt to lead to difficulties with interpretation. Some of these operated throughout the legislation and centred on the interpretation of words, phrases and definitions used in the Act. Some, however, related to specific parts of the legislation. We deal first with those aspects considered to be in need of more rigorous definition that operate throughout the Act.

The majority of these instances related to the use of words and phrases such as 'consult', 'challenge', 'take note of', 'observation', and 'reasonable', and apply to the majority of the provisions contained in the legislation. While it is recognised that much of English law is based on precedent and that many of these phrases may already have been considered and interpreted by the courts, there was an overwhelming view that in relation to this Act, they severely impaired its usefulness and effectiveness. Comments such as *"vague"* and *"wishy washy"* were made. Many also said that the Act gave every appearance of conferring rights, but in practice the legislation was sufficiently vague for these rights to be inoperable. In this context, these are the comments of one Brighton leaseholder:

> *"Though the Landlord and Tenant Act 1987 which came into operation some three years ago was widely welcomed as extending and strengthening the rights of tenants of privately owned flats, in practice it seems to have had only a limited effect."*

For the Act to be effective in providing solutions to landlord-tenant problems, it was felt that these issues were in urgent need of being addressed.

Similarly, where 'consultations' and 'observations' were allowed under the legislation, three issues arose. First, there was a general feeling that the nature of these observations and consultations should be more rigorously defined. Second, many felt that as the legislation currently stood landlords and managing agents could easily ignore tenants' views. Many of the respondents felt that there should be a statutory right to formal consultation with methods of redress where this was not complied with. Third, many felt that without time periods being prescribed in the Act, the legislation was wide open to abuse by the unscrupulous.

An issue of interpretation arose in relation to the definition of dwellings that are deemed to qualify under the Act (Section 20, paragraph 1; Section 5, paragraph 8). For the purposes of the legislation, do 'bed-sits' count as qualifying dwellings?

Turning now to more specific issues of interpretation, a small number of grey areas emerged that were related to discrete parts of the Act. These have already been discussed in Chapter 4, but are reviewed here. Most of the specific features that were felt to be open to interpretation centre on Section 42 of the Act and are concerned with the holding of service charge money in trust. The formation of 'trusts', the inclusion of 'sinking funds' under this section, and their operation either through separate bank accounts or accounting procedures were all issues that were raised. Where compliance with the legislation had incurred costs, the issue of who should pay for this was raised on a number of occasions, but not resolved to everyone's satisfaction. Whether Section 42 provided adequate protection against fraudulent use of service charge monies was also a moot point.

Three features of Part I of the Act (Right of first refusal) were felt to be in need of review. The first concerns the issue of roof space development. Does Part I apply when the freeholder sells the roof space for development purposes? In the two instances where this had arisen, the threat of court action had been sufficient to stop the proposed development in one instance; in the other the tenants objections were over-ruled and the landlord had the roof removed and a penthouse constructed. Even the professional advisors in the study held conflicting views as whether this was a legitimate practice. Tenants, overall, felt that where this was proposed they should have a statutory right to formal consultation; many of the managing agents and landlords did not agree, arguing that it was simply good business practice to develop existing assets. Second, the issue of whether Part I applied in cases where a head lease was being extended was also raised. While this is fully discussed in Chapter 4, the respondents were of the opinion that the legislation had complicated the process of extending head leases, because technically the freehold should now be offered to the tenants before the decision to extend it can be made.

The third grey area concerned the intention of Part I of the Act in relation to properties consisting of mixed commercial/residential use. The issue of whether Part I procedures should be triggered by floor space or commercial value was thought to be in need of review.

5.3 Sharp practices

Throughout the study tenants identified a large number of methods by which managing agents and landlords could frustrate the intentions of the legislation. Many of these might be considered to be 'sharp practices'; the majority refer to the provisions relating to service charges and estimates for work, although such practices also arose in connection with other provisions within the 1987 Act.

Service charges

In terms of service charges, some of these 'ruses' have been referred to earlier, namely: charging for inferior quality work; charging for items and services not provided; withholding service charge accounts; unexplained and unjustified increases in service charge demands; and the provision of 'too many' services in order to increase the managing agents fees. Additionally there were instances where managing agents were 'loading' the bills:

> *"the first managing agent we had was loading the bills, there was no doubt. Because I was checking up. We were getting photostats through and I was ringing [electricity board] and saying - you know, we've got those lights in the common parts that you press in and they come off; it's like a £150 a quarter, you know. So, I'd ring up and they'd say 'Oh no, that's not right. The bill is actually so and so.' And it was the same with the intercom."*
> (Leaseholder, Paddington)

A service charge issue arose in the course of discussion about variation of leases. This frequently mentioned sharp practice concerns the distribution of service charges when the landlord is also a tenant:

> *" ... a situation which is much more common where the landlord is throwing the expense of repairing his flat onto the other lessees, which is also, I think, very unjust. I mean, we got counsel's opinion on that and counsel was very hesitant but thought that probably we could succeed [in getting a deed of variation], but it certainly wasn't certain ... if the Act had been drafted to include that, as I think it should do, we should be able to get a variation of the lease so as to provide for a fairer distribution of service charges."*

It could be argued that in cases of disputed service charges such as these leaseholders always have recourse to court action. However, this course is not always easy and can be fraught with difficulty. Apart from the cost implications and delays involved in taking court action, there are other pitfalls:

> "[The managing agent] knows that the only avenue of redress lessees have is the law and that the cost of a case is almost always greater than the difference between their charges and a reasonable charge. They [the managing agents], via [the solicitors] always use the same tricks: they charge in advance to the service charge account for contested cases; when they lose they charge the service charge account. Lessees are given the idea that they are paying both [the managing agents'] costs and their own, whether they win or lose. When costs are awarded [the managing agent] charges to the service charge account the difference between the actual costs and the amount the court makes. Of course, these moves can be and are contested, but that means going back to court. [The managing agent] never perform a reasonable action without either a statutory obligation or a specific court order. [The managing agent] tries to get cases heard in the High Court, even where the amounts involved do not justify this, and always tries to avoid the actual issues of the case being discussed by tying up the case early on in technicalities - 'should this case be heard together or separately?', for example" (Leaseholder, Paddington; written notes provided with interview)

Many sharp practices were said to arise in connection with consultation over building estimates: tenants' estimates are lost in the post; spreading the cost of building works over a number of separate estimates in order that each one falls below the statutory level for consultation; letting contracts during the winter for external work and then charging for delays incurred; and accepting a low quotation and then charging for 'necessary extras'. These last two methods are said to be a way of increasing the managing agent's commission when fees are charged as a percentage of turnover. For example:

> "There is a collusion with the builders who do the major works, only in that both [the managing agent] and the builders know that the higher the price, the more each will receive so it is in the interests of both to push the costs up. This does not relate to the tendering process, but to later 'variations' which can amount ... to an additional 25% on top of the original figure quoted." (Leaseholder, Paddington)

Some managing agents were said to have other ways of increasing their commission by leaving minor works until they become urgent. For example, in one block of flats the managing agents were said to have delayed by 18 months the treatment of dry rot, increasing the cost from approximately £80,000 to an estimated £150,000.

Finally, in terms of service charges, one Brighton leaseholder told how a number of external works were carried out by the landlord which were paid for out of an insurance claim, yet the cost of the works were charged to the service charge account.

Insurance claims

Insurance claims were problematic. A small number of people had experienced difficulties in making a claim. In two instances the tenants found that the insurance company had been *"forbidden"* to talk to them. In another instance a claim made by one tenant was paid direct to the landlord. This was never reimbursed and the cost of the work was borne by the tenant herself. Perhaps the most frequently mentioned practice concerning buildings insurance, that was invariably viewed with distaste, was where the landlord and managing agents were paid commission by the insurance company. In such cases, it was argued, both the managing agent and the landlord stands to gain as fees are being paid twice: once by the insurance company to the landlord and again by the tenants through the service charge.

Variation of leases

Although tenants have the right to apply to the court for the variation of their lease, most people who considered this option did not pursue it on the grounds of costs. Some landlords were not averse to exploiting this fact, one solicitor told us. In exchange for payment, some landlords will agree to a change in the provisions of a lease; the payment required is usually a significant percentage less than the expected legal costs.

Right of first refusal

A number of practices that were considered devious and intended to deny the rights of tenants are concerned with the provisions of Part I of the 1987 Act. For example, Paragraph 4 (Section 21) allows the transfer of properties between associated companies. It was mentioned a number of times that 'paper' companies are set up whose sole aim is to own the freehold to a single property and appoint managing agents. In a number of instances it was known that the company owning the freehold and the management company were linked either financially, or by a common director, although this was said to be rarely admitted to in public. Where court action is taken against the landlord, for example for the appointment of a new managing agent, the property is transferred to an associated company which then re-appoints the existing agents to manage the property. The court action is foiled and the state of affairs over which the tenants took legal action continues. Invariably, the tenants who had experienced this said that they were penalised financially as they were unable to recoup any of their costs. This practice not only allows landlords to circumvent the law but also *"weakens the resolve"* and reduces the likelihood that tenants will attempt to take legal action again.

An alternative way of transferring properties without tenants purchasing the freehold involves inflating the sale price. In this case the directors were able to accomplish this by purchasing from their own company the freehold at an inflated price. The assets of the company (including the purchase price of the property) were then dissolved and returned to the directors. Should this be contested under Section 16 of Part I of the 1987 Act, the tenants would be obliged to purchase the property at an inflated price.

For example:

> *"I know of an instance where two joint owners of a property, which is only a freehold ground rent, wanted to dissolve the company which - it had held lots of properties - and they ended up with this tiny company with this ground rent worth £10,000 or something, and it wasn't worth keeping the company going. They were 50% shareholders and they wanted to just put it into their names and dissolve the company but there was no way they could do that without first offering it to the tenants .... what happened was that the directors of the company which was going to be dissolved set a very high price on the [freehold] - so that if for any reason anyone did catch up with them they would be able to sell it at a high price."* (Landlord, Paddington)

Because some landlords find the process laid down in Part I of the Act to be time consuming and expensive (in terms of interest lost on their capital), some resort to a different avoidance tactic. The new purchaser *"takes a chance"* when purchasing such a property:

> *"From a purchaser's point of view he will say to the vendor 'well I'll take my chances if you'll indemnify me against any legal fees that crop up'. So the purchaser says 'okay', and he takes his chance ... we have done that ... we have bought buildings where no notices have been served and we've just simply taken a chance."* (Landlord)

Those who had used such a ploy felt there was nothing illegal about this practice. However, they recognised that by not informing tenants of a change of landlord, many tenants may never realise that the landlord has changed. They are effectively denied their right of first refusal under the legislation.

Selling freeholds with conditions attached was also a technique described by some tenants. This usually arose where there had been prolonged disputes between the tenants and the companies that manage the building. In one case the opportunity to buy the freehold (under Part I) arose but was subject to the condition that the existing managing agent was retained. In another, the tenants asked the landlord to sell them the freehold, but again the same condition applied. In both cases, the tenants decided not to pursue the purchase any further.

Finally, a solicitor described a way of circumventing the right of first refusal by capitalising on legal jargon and people's ignorance of their rights. Having acted for both landlords and tenants, this is a practice that he had both seen as well as used himself. It makes use of Section 18 of the 1987 Act:

> *"... the legitimate way round the Act, and when I'm acting on a purchase what I normally get my clients to do if they'll go to the expense is the Section 18 clearance notice procedure, and that really pulls the rug out from under the feet of tenants ... you serve, under Section 18 a notice on the vast majority, if you can find them, of the qualifying tenants. There is no statutory form of notice, and there is no plain English form of notice so we just trot out what is in the section. You need to wrap a cold towel round your head to understand it and any tenant receiving it would not know what was going on ... if anybody needed a standard form or a prescripted form, we need one for Section 18 ... there are commercial forms available, all they do really is they follow the Act and they're incomprehensible.... the Act says you have to explain the effects of this section, which if you're not absolutely clear what the section says, you will set out the section ... the problem with Section 18 is that not only doesn't the qualifying tenant get the protected interest for a year, but they only get one month instead of two [to confirm their interest in purchasing the property] which is not a long time, particularly if you serve the notice around about Christmas time ... it's quite difficult for tenants if there's a number of them to get themselves together and put up a united front."* (Solicitor)

5.4 Loopholes
Information to be furnished to tenants

A small number of 'loopholes' were identified by which managing agents and landlords were felt to be able to either circumvent the law or render the intention of the provision ineffective. The first of these has been raised before and concerns the information that is to be furnished to tenants (Part VI). Section 48 (paragraph 1) states that 'A landlord of premises to which this Part applies shall by notice furnish the tenant with an address in England and Wales at which notices (including notices in proceedings) may be served on him by the tenant'. However, as many people pointed out, the ability to write to a landlord is ineffective in remedying any problems that might arise if the landlord chooses not to reply. While a landlord may comply with the legislation by providing a contact address, the legislation is rendered ineffective because there is no legal obligation to reply.

Right of first refusal

Three potential loopholes were identified by respondents with this part of the Act. The first concerns the ability of landlords to dispose of properties to members of the same family without being legally required to confer the right of first refusal under Part I of the 1987 Act (Section 4, paragraph 2, sub-section h). While it was generally recognised that it was, in principle, acceptable to allow the movement of assets between family members, a number of people pointed out that this provision is easily exploited by the unscrupulous. Although this section of the Act could be used in a number of ways, two specific scenarios were outlined. The first describes a situation in which tenants were pursuing court action over service charges. The action was addressed to a particular landlord and concerned gross overcharging for inferior quality work, together with discrepancies in the service charge accounts. The sums involved were said to be of the order of £10,000 over a period of two years. The day prior to the court hearing the landlord transferred the property, under Part I of the Act to a member of their family. The court action had to be halted because the original landlord no longer had a financial interest in the property. The tenants were unable to recoup their legal costs, and were unable, through lack of finances, to pursue the matter with the new landlord.

The second scenario arose in the discussion of the appointment of managers by the court and relates to the way in which the ownership of freeholds can be transferred under Part I (Right of First Refusal) of the Act. A Paddington leaseholder takes up the story and makes the following criticism:

> "we effectively don't have the right [to be consulted] because the landlord can easily evade it ... I would hope that consultation would be such that ... he'd take into account our requests ... the situation is this, first of all he's going to appoint the managing agents of his choice. Through the legislation we can challenge that, we will have to do it in the High Court, he will then be faced with proceedings in the High Court, probably take a year before the case was heard. Now I am contemplating what advice his lawyers would give him and I'm sure that advice would be two weeks before the hearing comes up in the High Court to change the freeholder to his son or his daughter or his brother-in-law, or something, and he would then file a declaration in the High Court, 'I am no longer the freeholder', case dismissed. So he would just cut the ground from under our feet completely ... this particular clause, clause 44 appears to be drawn up specifically to enable him to evade the consultation procedures by passing the property onto a new landlord, which would always have to be a family member of an associated company [under Part I]."

The second loophole to be identified in Part I of the Act allows freeholders to transfer properties between unassociated companies without requiring the right of first refusal to be conferred. A Paddington solicitor explains how this is done:

> "As yet, no step have been taken to close the loophole which allows shares in companies to be sold. In a significant number of cases, I have seen companies which own the freeholds of flats sell ownership of the company rather than sell the freehold. Technically there has been no change in landlord, although effectively the landlord has achieved exactly the same result as would have been achieved had the freehold been sold. This is a

loophole which is easily exploited and severely restricts operation of the right of first refusal provisions."

Third, a potential loophole exists where the right of first refusal is not conferred and tenants pursue corrective action. Although tenants are entitled to purchase the property from the new landlord, there is said to be no legal obligation in the 1987 Act for the new landlord to sign a contract transferring the freehold to the tenants. For example:

"... if you have not applied to the court within three months of your serving your purchase notice on the new landlord, then you may lose your right if a binding contract hasn't been entered into. Now I think that whoever drafted the procedure here envisaged that the tenants having served a notice would mess around over actually entering into the contract, of course the opposite is actually the case, the tenants want to buy, they've served the purchase notice and it can be a damn awful business getting the new owner to sign. There's nothing here that says he has to sign a contract. So he can dither about. So you make your application to the court, you have your hearing before the court and then in sub-section 4 of [paragraph] 17 'if a period of two months beginning with the date of the determination of that application has expired and no binding contract has been entered into between the new landlord and the nominated person, and no other such application as mentioned under Section 3(b) is pending, then again the owner can serve on you a notice saying this Act no longer applies.' So it means having got your court order it is meaningless... As far as I can see it's a very defective section. I don't know what you do with your purchase notice; I don't know how you can enforce it [the sale] because again it's subject to contract." (Solicitor)

5.5 Summary

Many people initially welcomed the Landlord and Tenant Act 1987 as it gave every indication that it would strengthen the rights of tenants of privately owned flats and provide a means to resolve disputes arising between tenants, landlords, and their appointed agents. While there is a general view from all parties that the Act has much to commend it, in principle at least, its effectiveness in practice is seriously impaired. This is primarily for four reasons. First, the Act is felt to have a number of procedural deficiencies and lacks sufficient powers to enforce compliance with the Act's provisions. Second, the legislation includes a number of 'grey areas', some of which are specific to individual parts of the Act, others operating throughout the Act. The use of vague and undefined terms are included in this category. Third, landlords and managing agents were said to use a range of sharp practices. Some of these are used to circumvent the law, others are intended to stop or reduce the likelihood of tenants taking legal action. Finally, the Act includes a small number of loopholes including three which allow freeholders to evade conferring the right of first refusal (Part I).

Chapter 6   Leaseholding and Related Management Issues

In this chapter we examine a number of factors which are not directly related to the Landlord and Tenant Act 1987, but have implications for the practice of leasehold management, in general, and for the way in which people are able to resolve management difficulties, in particular.

The resolution of management problems is one of the main intentions of the 1987 Act. We have seen in previous chapters that for a variety of reasons, there are certain deficiencies within the legislation which impair its effectiveness. There are also external factors which have the same effect. Four main issues emerged. First, few leaseholders were explicitly aware of their rights and duties under the terms of their leases. This was said to give rise to expectations that were sometimes in excess of the landlords' or the managing agents' stated duties. Second, the ability to resolve management problems often depends on a person being able to establish their rights and pursue them through legal means. Considerable comment was made about the availability and readability of relevant materials designed to inform people of their rights.

The third issue concerns court action - few people were willing to take court action, in part because of a fear of the unknown, and in part because of the potential expense. Fourth, in terms of management practices it has already been pointed out in the previous chapter that unscrupulous landlords and agents may employ a variety of sharp practices to the detriment of leaseholders. There are three issues that relate to the way in which property managers conduct their business affairs that are of concern when considering the relationship between tenants, landlords and their appointed agents; the calculation of management fees, the issue of professional status, as recognised through a governing professional body, and the potential need for professional indemnity.

6.1 Understanding leases and 'leasehold'

Buying leasehold properties was sometimes described as being much more complex than buying a freehold property. This was partly because of the nature of the contract that was being entered into and partly due to perceived difficulties in ascertaining details of the management history of the flat.

Leasehold

A number of leaseholders commented that when they first bought their property they had little idea of the contract they were entering to; inevitably they simply felt they were buying a flat with little understanding of the associated implications.

> "You need a place to live. You've moved job or whatever; you've got a certain time to do it in; you're in this problem of trying to sell your old place and getting a new one. And you're looking for a flat, and you start going round the district and some of them are so grotty and so terrible you wouldn't think of putting a dog in there, and eventually you find the one which you think is possible. Unfortunately it doesn't then become a clinical judgement, It's the place that you want and it's going to cost you quite a lot of money with the mortgage and everything else. When this stuffy solicitor says 'well you know there is a thing about common drains', you think what the hell's he talking

about, I'm not bothered with that. You want a flat, come on, get on with it.
All too often, they don't realise. [It's not] until the service charges come in
and he starts knocking the place about, putting something on the roof and
that, that they realise that the lease which they signed they should have read,
and which their solicitor should have gone through with them and, you know,
explained what all this means, and what they're in for. They hadn't the
interest at the time of buying, it only comes to them later." (Leaseholder,
Paddington)

Due to a lack of interest or opportunity to familiarise themselves with the terms of
their lease, many leaseholders were said to be unaware of either the landlord's or
their own duties.

This was said to be a major cause of concern as it often meant that tenants had
unrealistic expectations of the landlord's duties. For example, both managing
agents and landlords indicated a number of ways in which they were expected to
remedy problems that were not stated in the lease. Issues such as handling
insurance claims under an individual person contents' insurance, dealing with
noisy neighbours, and caring for the garden when this was not covered by the
service charge were mentioned. *"Anything you can think of, they will ask you to do*
it", said one managing agent.

A lack of familiarity with leaseholding, in general, also meant that tenants were
sometimes unaware of the extent to which service charges were likely to rise, or
indeed their requirement to contribute to a sinking fund. *"It came as quite a shock"*,
recalled one leaseholder of a converted apartment.

Out of this arises the issue of whose responsibility it is to educate and inform people
about the nature of leaseholding. Inevitably, it is the responsibility of the parties
who sign the lease to be aware of the implications of their actions:

> *"The essence of the thing is that the lease is the contract. It's signed by the*
> *landlord, it's signed by the leaseholder and this is something that I keep*
> *bashing away at them all the time. You've signed this contract, you haven't*
> *even bothered to read the bloody thing. When I ask you questions about it,*
> *you don't even know what's there."* (Barrister)

It was acknowledged, however, that the technical nature of leases meant that most
lay people would require assistance in understanding the intricacies of leases. Some
people felt that it was the duty of either the landlord or the managing agent to
perform this role; it was pointed out, however, that the unscrupulous could have a
vested interest in misinforming or withholding certain information. A more widely
held view was that solicitors (or conveyancers) should assume this role. In cases
where this had happened, respondents said that they felt much more aware and
confident about the practice of leaseholding and the content of their leases. Many
of the respondents, from all parties concerned, felt that solicitors and estate agents
should have a statutory duty to inform potential buyers of the nature of owning a
leasehold property.

Despite being informed of the contents of a lease and its implications, a potential
buyer, it was felt, still had little information about how the property had been
managed in the past, and the present incumbents relationship with the landlord or
their agent. For example:

> *"Unless it's a new property what you're buying from the existing leaseholder*
> *is a long lease. Now he's not going to tell you [about any problems] because*

he wants to sell, he'll keep very quiet about it. What's the landlord like? Oh, he's very good, you know, he's a very helpful chap." (Leaseholder, Paddington)

Although this was mentioned only a few times the urgency with which this was discussed suggested that it was an area in need of review. Few people had any concrete solutions to this dilemma; one leaseholder, however, felt that it should be standard practice for potential buyers to receive, through their solicitors, copies of the service charge accounts for the previous five years. In addition, potential buyers should have access to the details of any legal action that had risen in connection with the existing managing agent and landlord.

Leases

In this section we discuss people's views about the nature and format of leases and discuss a number of suggestions that emerged.

Leases were almost universally claimed to be vague, open to interpretation and difficult to understand. *"Gobbledegook"* was an expression often applied to the format and content of leases.

> *"It is a legal document. And as such it's structured on legal precedent, and where the 'commas' and the 'ands' or 'buts' are is significant in a court of law. But it's confusing."* (Advisor)

> *"They are complicated because they're trying to deal with so many things .....every lease has got to have variations in it to take account of the peculiarities in the building and the people who are going to be in there ... But I mean, you spend hours just finding the right provision. You know, the provision for repairs might be on the first page in one lease and on the first schedule or the eighth schedule on another lease, and it's just a waste of time really. I do think a lot of leases are very badly drafted."* (Advisor)

> *"... the forfeiture clause. It has to be there if you want to go for non-payment of rent. It actually says that if the rent isn't paid within 14 days the landlord or his agent has the right to re-enter. He doesn't have any such right at all. It's gobbledegook. But unless you say that, you go to court and if the judge doesn't see it he'll throw you out."* (Advisor)

The problem with the nature of leases is threefold: first, leases are written in a technical language that is difficult to understand for the lay person, and on occasions for the legal profession too;

> *"They [leases] can be terribly complex and impenetrable, even my legal advisor has had a problem with some of them."* (Landlord)

Second, leases are often said to be vague or silent about many of the rights and duties that both tenants and landlords have come to expect:

> *".. there's lots of things leases don't mention but they should do; whose responsibility are the windows, you know, maintenance, are they internal and therefore the tenants or external and the landlords; maintenance funds, collecting service charge arrears, because we have had a few of those in the past; the right to discuss the service charges; where the AGM [for the property company] is held so we can discuss the accounts ... you mention it, its bound not to be in one of our leases."* (Leaseholder living in a 1950s built block of flats and chairman of a residents association.)

Third, leases are sometimes felt to be written in such a way that they become subject to interpretation:

> "*Unfortunately not all the leases are as clear as they may be. Then you get into barristers' opinions and solicitors, etc.. as to the way they interpret it ... Once you start getting into that, you know full well that it's too vague to go to court and really argue about. You're better to stay out and say 'Well, look, can he come to some agreement on this?'.*" (Leaseholder)

> "*You do get big problems and the biggest of all of them, which people don't seem to worry about ... where the flat isn't properly defined. Nobody knows where one flat finishes and the next one starts, and whose responsibility for doing it [works] and who's got to pay for it.*" (Solicitor)

> "*... the archaic language is really daft ... the clauses would be about that long after all the 'whoevers', and 'notwithstandings', and 'appertaining to's' have been taken out. You shouldn't have them ... come on stop speaking this archaic language. If you're not allowed to hang clothes out of the window, just say so. All you need to say is - 'You are not allowed to hang clothes out of the window'. I think that's quite straightforward.*" (Advisor)

Overwhelmingly, respondents felt that the nature and format of leases needed attending to. After all, as a number of managing agents argued, if the lease is open to interpretation it makes management of the building much more difficult and open to dispute.

In considering possible solutions, no one suggested that 'antiquated' leases should be swept aside overnight. However, but there was a considerable body of opinion indicating that greater efforts should be made towards revising the format, language and content of leases. Overall, respondents felt that leases should conform to three main principles: they should be clear and understandable to all parties; the terms of the lease should be comprehensive with a full statement of responsibilities on both sides; and nothing should be allowed into a lease that is vague or requires any form of interpretation.

Two main solutions to the problems of 'unreadable' and 'vague' leases were proposed that conform to these principles. First, the vagueness of leases could be addressed by requiring, by statute, all new leases to be written in plain English. A suggested alternative would be to retain a short lease in the current 'antiquated' format but with schedules and/or 'translations' provided that convey the essence of the lease in plain English. For example:

> "*It would be nice if solicitors in conveyancing could take that lease and run it through his wordprocessor, and provide a supplement so that it actually talks about what the obligations are. Rather than 'as the vendee; the vendor; first rights of the second clause, para three'. So it could be fed out so a guy who buys a flat can then say 'Oh I know I've got to do that and that and that, this is what's gonna happen. I can sub-let my flat, service charges are allowed under the terms of the lease, etc.'. He has a complete knowledge of what's in there, obligations and commitments.*" (Advisor)

Considerable progress towards plain English leases could be made, it was thought by one advisor, by drawing up a standard lease, with a range of standard clauses that could be used as and when necessary. New clauses, in plain English, could be written to cover less frequently occurring eventualities. A number of managing agents, landlords and advisors agreed with this position and suggested that various bodies including the Law Commission, the Law Society, the Royal Institute of Chartered Surveyors, and the Department of the Environment, could get together, if they were not already doing so, to reform leases in this way.

The second solution relates to the perceived 'incompleteness' of leases. Leases, it was generally felt, should include a full statement of the obligations and commitments of all parties signing. Two respondents give an example of their perceptions of the coverage of good leases; first a solicitor, second a managing agent:

> "When I look through a lease what I'm looking for is that it's got all the necessary rights of access, support and shelter, and that the premises are clearly defined and are in accordance with what you think, or your client thinks they're getting; that there are adequate arrangements for the repair of the structure and common parts, and cleaning and lighting of the common parts ... that there is provision for the freeholder to enforce the covenants of the lease against the other tenants ... that means that if you've got five leases in a house, you want the landlord to make sure that they're all identical so they all sort of work in the same way and that they're all covered by the same sort of regulations." (Solicitor)

> "I think a good lease from a managing agent's point of view has to encompass good service charge clauses. What do I mean by that? Probably for means of administration half yearly .... so I would like to see half yearly interim service charges in advance, with interest charged on arrears when not paid in the period by lessees. With provision to be made in the lease that in the event of some urgent expenditure occurring, then the lease does provide for an additional interim service charge to be demanded ... if you've got a foreign resident, how do you take action for non-payment of service charge .... it's got to make provision for a security deposit and an address for service of notice within this country ... you should be able to provide for [the recovery of legal costs] if you instruct solicitors." (Managing agent)

Tenants who had cause to look at their lease felt that they were often very one-sided. Leases mainly seemed to be concerned with the landlord's rights, for example rents, service charges and the forfeiture of leases in cases of non-payment, rather than their duties. Most respondents felt that the coverage of leases should be reviewed and include a schedule of the landlord's obligations. For example, clauses concerning the maintenance of the fabric of the building and of the common parts should be included. In addition, provision should be made for sinking funds, protection against rapidly escalating service charges, formal consultation (both written and in person) over the use of service charge monies, and adequate protection against the provision of inadequate or inferior services.

6.2 Access to relevant information

In this section we discuss an issue that frequently arose during the interviews, the availability of information about the Landlord and Tenant Act 1987, in particular, and housing legislation, in general. We discuss first, people's experience of trying to find suitable information, second, the nature of the information required, and third, suggested methods of making relevant information available.

Gaining access to relevant information

Managing agents, solicitors, and to some extent other advisors generally found no difficulties in obtaining information about new legislation. This was usually supplied either by their professional bodies or through their subscription to professional reference publications. There were some comments, however, about delays before information about new legislation filtered down to them.

Tenants, however, almost universally said that suitable information was very difficult to obtain. Landlords also expressed similar views. Here are two leaseholders expressing their views about the availability of relevant information.

> *"People don't know their rights and even if they did they wouldn't quite know how to go about it; there's no one to tell them"* (Leaseholder, Manchester)

> I: Did you feel the need for advice from somewhere?"

> R: "Yes. I mean it got quite desperate. I felt desperate at times. You just feel so helpless." (Leaseholder, Croydon)

It was pointed out in an earlier chapter that it is very common for people to operate on a 'need to know' basis. It is only in times of crisis that they look for the relevant information. While there were a small number of people who were able to search out the information they required, the majority felt very poorly informed. It is interesting to note that many of the tenants said they felt better informed of their rights after attending one of the group discussions; many also requested copies of the synopses of the Act used to generate discussions (Appendix E). This included many people who had experienced problems with their managing agent or landlord, and in some cases had taken action.

Against a background of generally low awareness about the 1987 Act, in the next sections we discuss the nature of respondents' information needs and the issue of how information should be distributed.

Information needs

It was generally recognised that the balance between comprehensiveness and complexity is not easy to achieve. However, many people felt that the current choice of obtaining a copy of the 1987 Act and a DoE publication left considerable room for improvement. There was a general view that much of the information currently available was not specific enough - *"it's written for Mr and Mrs average"*. Some people had seen the booklets produced by the Department of the Environment. Most felt that they were limited in scope. One managing agent referred to them as *"noddy guides"* that were written in such a way as to *"be deceptive to use as they don't cover every right, and omit key pieces of the legislation"*.

Most respondents wanted information that was concise, easy to read, comprehensive, and relevant to them and their housing needs. A plea was also made on a number of occasions for suitable housing information to be provided in languages other than English.

In terms of the legislation, many professionals felt that the 1987 Act was far less readable than housing legislation in general. In part, this was because it was felt to have been badly structured and poorly drafted:

> *"It's apparent if you're a lawyer reading it [that it was] passed before it was ready ... the Act is badly structured, there are definitions in the main body and in the schedules ... they should all be in the schedules ... and without very very careful reading you don't know where the definitions change, because they do change as you work through the Act."*

The 1987 Act was also thought to be particularly complicated because it consisted of a mix of new legislation and amendments to existing law. Indeed, many advisors and managing agents said that, particularly in terms of the service charge provisions, these could only be used if both the 1985 and 1987 Landlord and Tenant Acts were comprehensibly cross-referenced. This was said to have made interpretation much more complicated. The opportunity should have been taken, it was felt by many, to *"strike through the legislation and start again"*:

> *"Why they didn't consolidate the '85 and '87 Act I don't know. It would have made good sense and stopped some of the silly omissions and loopholes. They might have got the structure better too. They've duplicated things too. If Section 42 is about trusts we don't need all this about how to set them up. There is ample tried and tested trust law already. But my main beef is that it is so badly put together with definitions here, there, and there. You know, it's one of those nightmare Acts .... well you need both Acts [1985 and 1987] don't you, or else you don't know where you are. They should have consolidated them together."* (Landlord, Paddington)

*Distributing
information*
Tenants

Many people felt that very little effort, if any at all, was made to communicate the content of new legislation. Almost without exception this was felt to be totally inadequate. The issue arises of how to distribute information to relevant individuals. Two quite different, but complementary approaches were suggested: a general distribution of information to the population as a whole, versus the targeting of information to individuals to whom the legislation would have relevance. We discuss these in turn.

Many people favoured a general broadcast of information through the various media:

> *"Television is an interesting option [to use], whether by way of case studies or adverts. I can see a kind of documentary principle going through on the TV, on how individual people can go about using the various legislation. An interesting analogy is buying shares. Up to five years ago it was unheard of. To sell off the Electricity shares, all of the sudden people had to be, you know, they had to put it on television and they had to make people aware of what you do have and, you know ... that had the benefit of getting of five million people ... It's the same with flats isn't it, and the Act, why not get five million people behind that?"* (Leaseholder, Paddington)

Television was thought to be the best media for generally informing people of the rights. Many respondents also felt that this should be supplemented, as is the current practice, by producing information leaflets and booklets that are available through outlets such as libraries, CABx, local authorities, etc. Other worthwhile suggestions including the placing of informative adverts on buses, tube trains, and billboards.

The second suggested way of publicising legislation involves targeting a specific audience. While it was recognised that contacting individual leaseholders would be a virtually impossible task, three suggestions for targeting relevant information emerged. The first two suggestions concern the distribution of information to existing leaseholders, the third suggestion to new leaseholders. First, many, but by no means all, leaseholders are members, either individually or through their residents association, of local or national organisations that seek to promote the rights of leaseholders. These organisations, it was thought, could voluntarily register with the Department; whenever new legislation occurred bulletins or fact sheets could be mailed direct to the organisation for distribution to individual members. A model for such practice already exists in other government departments (eg DSS). It was suggested that grant-aid may need to be made available in some cases.

Second, a freephone telephone number could be advertised nationally for individuals to use to obtain relevant publications.

Third, it was argued many times that the most appropriate time to inform potential leaseholders of their rights was at the time of purchase. Many thought that this could be accomplished through solicitors, conveyancers, mortgage lenders, and estate agents. For example:

> *"I think that part of it could be done by the estate agents because a lot of estate agents sell leasehold flats. I am a great believer in if you set yourself up as a profession, as estate agents do, then you have a duty of care to whoever you're selling or renting to - to both sides. To your purchaser and your vendor ... there's a duty of care there."* (Advisor)

> *"The trouble is that there is self interest and they don't really want to point out the snags, do they. The estate agents want to sell a lease, the property owner wants to sell a lease, or the previous owner of the lease wants to sell the lease ... I think that probably solicitors are the best party to inform them."*(Advisor)

Managing agents and landlords were not generally considered to be the most appropriate people through whom information could be conveyed. This was primarily because a conflict of interest could arise. Managing agents and landlords were generally in agreement with this. However, one landlord, with a policy of allowing existing tenants to purchase the freehold of the building under the 1987 Act, did provide a copy of the relevant DoE publication to each individual tenant. This was viewed by tenants in a generally favourable light.

It was very apparent that resident-owned management companies were often not aware of their duties under the 1987 Act. This was felt to have potentially serious implications and an issue that required urgent attention.

Managing agents and landlords

Managing agents were generally satisfied with the information they received about new legislation. In general this was obtained through their professional bodies. However, grey areas in the legislation which were open to interpretation meant that sometimes there were delays in receiving this information from their professional bodies.

Landlords, however, were often not aware of their legal duties. This was of concern to many of the respondents. Some landlords felt that it was the duty of their solicitors to advise them on their legal duties and points of law. Others, however, felt it was the landlords' duty to keep informed of new and changing legislation. While recognising it was not the government's role to do this, there was a feeling that government departments could assist the take-up of information. For example:

> *"I think one of the pitfalls of most professions is that you don't actually get bulletins - from DoE, or whoever - on current legislation and we only find out either through word of mouth or through publications ... That's one of the pitfalls of the new Act. We don't hear about them ... the government has*

got an obligation, obviously, to keep the world at large informed, and the professions, but I don't think there's any basis on which the government can have any obligations to make sure that I am informed about something ... but I wouldn't mind being on a register and for bulletins or information sent to me direct. That would be very sensible indeed." (Landlord - Property developer)

6.3 Taking legal action

This section considers four issues: people's experiences of taking court actions; views about taking court action; the reasons why some people do not use court action to this method of resolve landlord-tenant problems; and the suggested alternatives to taking court action.

Experiences of taking court action

Few people had taken court action. While some had won their cases, most were not pleased with the overall outcome or the process by which it had been accomplished. The process of taking court action was almost always said to be a major burden. Three reasons were given: the amount of time a person had to spend putting a case together, the delays in getting to court, and the expense of taking the action. Here are a few respondents describing their experiences:

The time involved

"... it took me seven months of evenings and weekends to prepare a dossier of the [bad] management ... that included consulting all the professionals and getting this file together." (Leaseholder, conversion)

"It's horrendous. I mean, when I'd finished preparing for my case - I'll show you the documents, the file I prepared for my counsel, it's huge... when I'd finished preparing this stuff, most of this is correspondence with some sort of explanation on the first few pages, and that took me as long to do as [to write] a novel." (Leaseholder, mansion block)

Delays

"You've nerved yourself up, you've done all your homework, you've burned the midnight oil, you've briefed your barrister, your solicitor, your surveyor and everything, you've got all the people there, they've cancelled holidays and meeting, you go there, you sit through a day in court, your case is never heard, it goes on to the next day, and then you finally come to it, then there's the hearing ... sometimes if it's complex you won't get a decision on the day, he will give judgement later ... then the question of costs, they've got to be taxed, they can be opposed. Months and months and months later you might get a settlement." (Leaseholder, conversion)

"It took 18 months to get to court, the agents kept petitioning for postponement on technicalities, and then when you go to court, there isn't the court time available to go through all these procedures." (Leaseholder, conversion)

Expense

"It's commitment and it's money, you need to spend money as well, and you need excellent professional people to assist you because they will put good people up against you. You might think he's an absolute villain, this landlord, but he'll put a good barrister and a surveyor up against you, and you've got to counter that with the best you can get." (Leaseholder, conversion. Current estimated costs of £90,000.)

"It is so expensive, I just can't afford to go to court anymore, none of us can, we've been bled dry." (Leaseholder, mansion block)

"Another couple just gave in because they said 'we can't have the problem of having a legal case, and the cost of one. It's too much, it's too much anxiety and expense." (Leaseholder, mansion block)

Views about taking court action

Court action was rarely seen as the best way of resolving housing problems. This was for four main reasons: difficulties with financing court action and re-couping legal costs; the unpredictable nature of court action; the inability to fight 'class actions'; and problems with using the County Court. We consider these in turn.

The potential expense of court action was the major cause of difficulty for tenants in seeking legal redress. Apart from the scale of the expense - *'escalating'* was how one tenant described it - problems of finding sufficient money 'upfront', and the likelihood of only being able to recoup a proportion of the costs incurred were mentioned. For example:

Financing court action

"Lots of money, not small money, you're talking four figure sums. And you've got to put that up front. Alright you may get your costs back or most of your costs back at the end of the day, but that's at the end of the day. You've got to put your money up front." (Leaseholder, conversion)

Recouping legal costs

"You are lucky if you get 60% of your costs back, even if you win the case ... they can oppose the costs line by line ... so when you start putting money out for legal cases, okay, well if you get damages that'll offset it to some extent, but on costs you can say bye-bye to over half of it, unless you're very lucky". (Leaseholder/Barrister)

Second, embarking on court action was often thought to be a risk: partly because of the 'tricks' that managing agents and landlords can use, but also partly because of the unpredictable nature of court action itself.

It has been argued that if a tenant who takes legal action is 'in the right' then any expenses that are incurred will be recouped. However, there are two reasons why this is not so.

• **It is not unknown for cases to be withdrawn just prior to the court hearing:**

"... the final thing they do when they know they're going to lose, they take you right up to the day you're going to court, and they will settle out of court. They will just pay up or say 'we agree', and of course you have to bear all the costs incurred to take it to that stage." (Leaseholder, conversion)

• **Being 'in the right' does not guarantee a successful outcome:**

"Nobody is this world is ever sure when they go to court that they're going to win. It's an adversarial system and quite often the one who wins is not the own with the best case, it's the way in which it is presented. In other words, has he got a good barrister and solicitor. If you've got a better barrister, solicitor and surveyor on the opposing side, you will lose, no matter how good your case is because you can't get it across to the judge, and he's going

to take note of what the better presented side has to say." (Leaseholder, conversion)

A third issue arose in the discussion of taking legal action which relates to the efficiency with which the law is thought to tackle housing and related problems. It concerns residents associations, who often felt that they should be able to take action collectively rather than having to put forward an individual. This is very difficult to arrange, as one tenant described:

> *"If you want to get somebody legally to represent you in such a case, where do you go to? There's no legal body [that] can represent residents' associations. They represent individuals. It comes down to a case rather than a class action. We wanted to get a solicitor to represent us in what was a class action. They don't like messing around with residents associations because it's a very amorphous thing ... you really don't have anywhere to go. I talked to [local council] about these things 'Who can I talk to? Who'll do these sorts of things?', they said, 'no there isn't anybody'. There's this big black hole. The legislation's there for your protection, but nobody's there to ensure you can be protected."* (Leaseholder, mansion block)

The fourth issue concerns the use of the County Court to resolve housing issues. As another tenant argued "there's no precedent set in the county court, it's a thorough waste of time continually debating the same issues". The consequence is that, because no legal precedents are set in the County Court, the same issues can repeatedly be debated. Because rulings on similar issues were thought to vary from case to case, unscrupulous managing agents and landlords were said to use this threat of court action to their advantage and force tenants to comply with their wishes.

Reasons for not taking court action

A number of tenants in the study had contemplated taking legal action primarily over problems of service charges or poorly completed work. The reasons they gave for not pursuing this course of action were threefold: unfamiliarity with the process of court action; the feeling that court action was generally a last resort and only for major problems; and the potential cost of court action. For example:

- **Nervous of taking court action**

  "I just wouldn't know where to start ... it just doesn't seem to be the sort of thing I would do." (Leaseholder, Brighton)

  "You've got to be joking, I'd be terrified." (Leaseholder, Brighton)

- **Worried about possible repercussions**

  ".. the big thing is that a lot of them don't want to give evidence. They don't want to cross swords with their landlord in court because they think it might prejudice them in the future, whatever the result." (Solicitor)

- **Court seems inappropriate**

  "... my problem is over £100 service charge bill ... why go to court over that ... there must be an easier way." (Leaseholder, Manchester)

84

"Now you've mentioned the insurance, I would like my insurance certificate ... I've been trying again to get it, but I couldn't go to court for it." (Leaseholder, Paddington)

- **The cost of court action**

  "We did consider it [going to court] but it was cheaper to have the work done again." (Leaseholder, Paddington)

  "I know what court costs are like ... there's no way we could afford it ... and we wouldn't get Legal Aid." (Leaseholder, Brighton)

Alternatives to court action

Many people recognised the difficulties and expense of taking court action. Many felt that there needed to be a different solution. Some of these centred around a local ombudsman or housing court that would have the jurisdiction to settle landlord-tenant disputes;

"I like the idea of having a housing court ... there must be so many problems that there would be enough work for them ... they would have specialist knowledge too." (Landlord, Brighton)

"A tribunal would be good; it would be informal, not as expensive and not as intimidating as court." (Leaseholder, Brighton)

An alternative that used the Lands Tribunal was also suggested:

"I think court action is the last thing everybody wants. Perhaps a tribunal like the Lands Tribunal might be more appropriate. The Consumer Council is an interesting idea, they're a people-friendly body that people can approach. Of course, the big problem is that if you have a problem with a television, it's not worth a great deal of money. If you have a problem with your rent on a flat it is worth a lot of money. So there's that bridge to cross. People do not like to approach solicitors, they cost a great deal of money." (Leaseholder, mansion block)

However, some concern was expressed about the viability of such alternatives to court. In part this was because of cost. However, there was also a view that tribunals or local courts would not have sufficient jurisdiction, and would soon become overwhelmed by the volume of cases:

"I don't think any other forum has the authority or a court ... tribunals can become as formal and as complicated as courts themselves ... I think developments are in another direction ... in the new justice review there was a proposal in that for a specialist housing court. Now that was actually turned down, but at the same time the jurisdiction of the county court is being altered a little so that the county court can hear claims of a much higher value ... and starting from next April there is going to be what's called a housing action in the county court, but before the registrar, so in a more informal setting and not on adversarial system that you see in court, more of an inquisitional one ... I think that's probably the way to go." (Local Authority Housing Advisor)

The issue of how disputes should be settled is open to be debate. However, the views that strongly emerge from these discussions are that whatever system is adopted it should address the two main problems currently experienced by tenants, notably the cost of resolving disputes and the delays in obtaining a hearing.

6.4 Managing agents - practices and fees

The issue of how managing agents conduct their business was raised a number of times by all parties concerned. Two main issues arise for discussion. The first concerns the regulation of management practices, the second concerns management fees.

Management practices

It was noted in Chapter 2 that many of the tenants who took part in stage one of the study had not experienced any problems of management whilst living in their current flat. Many felt that they had a good relationship with their managing agent; others had no cause for concern. However, there were a number of people who had experienced major problems with the managing agents instructed by the landlord to look after the block. A solicitor describes the practices of one of these managing agents:

> "... the problems arise if you've got, as I had with my two mansion blocks, the situation where the freeholder, the managing agents the builders, the quantity surveyor, the architects and all the rest of it are actually in business together. They go around the country buying up blocks that need refurbishment, they charge a Rolls Royce price for doing everything they possibly can to the block ... the look for a block that's in need of refurbishment and they go in and they rip the tenants off as far as I'm concerned, and then of course they fight tooth and nail over getting the management withdrawn from them, until they're ready, and then they just cave in ... it can go on for years and years and years .... they've [managing agents] repealed every order the registrar made and sometimes made second appeals back to the Judge himself, and on one they threatened to appeal to the Court of Appeal ... In the meantime of course, demands were going out to the tenants for management fees on the basis of the work they were having to do to protect themselves from the litigation and legal fees. We had £60,000 a year in legal fees being charged to us." (Solicitor)

Most of the managing agents felt that scenarios such as this should not happen. They felt that this harmed tenant-managing agent relations and brought the profession into disrepute.

Although not the view of all the managing agents in the study , it was generally felt that the practices of managing agents should be overseen by a professional body, in the same way as doctors, lawyers, and surveyors. Indeed, many said that they would like to see a professional body with a professional code of conduct to which managing agents would be required to adhere to. There were some dissenters to this view: some felt that as most managing agents were either chartered surveyors or estate agents by profession, membership of their own professional bodies should be sufficient. However, despite this there was also the view that as managing agents had received considerable 'bad press' in recent years a professional body that represented their interests would be generally beneficial.

Leaseholders, in general, supported the notion that, at the very least, managing agents should adhere to a formal code of practice. Most of the managing agents in the study were not averse to this. Leaseholders, and many of the advisors felt that managing agents should be required, by statute, to register with a professional body. Managing agents were less keen on this idea, and felt that voluntary registration was sufficient.

Similarly, there was some suggestion that managing agents should conform to a code of practice to which disciplinary procedures were attached; managing agents, in general, preferred the notion of self-regulation. A leaseholder and advisor puts forward his view:

> *"I'm a leaseholder too, they take my money on trust. I wouldn't normally give money to anyone I didn't know something about. The investment industry has their watchdogs, you know, FIMBRA, and so on. Why shouldn't managing agents be bound by the same sort of governing body. They should be like other professionals. They should register and have professional indemnity ... I, for one, would feel a lot happier."* (Advisor, Croydon)

A managing agent responds:

> *"There is no need for all that [guidelines and registration]. It just makes everything less efficient bureaucratic. Some of us are already regulated by RICS."*

Management fees

An issue that was repeatedly raised by all respondents was that of management fees. Many of the leaseholders were not happy about the way in which fees were calculated. In part this was due to leaseholders being unaware of the work that managing agents carry out - *"when it goes smoothly, it appears we never do anything, and then some people start to complain"*, responded one managing agent - but also in part to the practices which some managing agents adopt in calculating their fees.

Some managing agents charge a flat fee per unit for residential management; others charge a percentage of the turnover of the service charge account; yet others, use a combination of the two methods. The biggest problems were said to arise when the managing agent charges a percentage of the turnover as a fee. It is here that unscrupulous practices can occur. Chapter 2 described how some agents were said to overspend on the service charge account by providing 'unnecessary' building works or services, or else delaying work until the scale of the work changed from minor to major. The overall effect of this was to inflate the management fee. However, even when bad practices are not involved, this method of charging was still felt to be unfair:

> *"the managing agent orders a thousand gallons of fuel and charges x% and gets x pounds from it. He makes one phone call. He orders ten thousand gallons of oil and charges x% and gets ten times x pounds for the same phone call. I call that unfair and unjustified."* (Tenant, Brighton)

How should fees be calculated? Most tenants felt that a flat fee was the most appropriate. Where 'additional duties' were separately required these should be agreed and paid for from the service charge account. Managing agents were rather more varied in their views. Some felt that a *"percentage is fair because it's the nature of the business"*, while others preferred a flat fee arrangement. This is one managing agent's solution to the problem of fees:

> *".. as managing agents we are told specifically what's expected of us by the landlord, but what the landlord may expect us to do and what the tenants may expect us to do may be totally different things. But if there is one common written document whereby we've got all our cards on the table, and say right, that's what we undertake to do for this fee, there'd be no question of problems because if we do not perform, we get sacked. If it is agreed that for a certain*

list of duties that we've agreed and signed, ... that we get a certain fee, then there shouldn't be any problem with that. They should pay the fee. If they do not want us to perform certain duties, then we can delete a few of them and the fee is reduced ... if we know specifically what we're expected to do - which most managing agents don't, they [leases] should be very specific - that's the way we would like to see it. That way we have a list of tasks which are a) agreed by the landlord, b) counter agreed by the residents association. Once we're given that task it's up to us to come back and say what our fee for that particular job would be ... we perhaps can have like a 5 star type fee, and a four star, or three star type service whereby tenants say, 'well actually we don't want all these things, we only want you to do the very basic things', and the fee's different, because it requires a different time input. All this is essentially based on time, not on turnover of service charges or the number of flats in a building.... anything on top of that then we can separately quote for it ... if it were up to me, I'd bring either guidelines or legislation [in] which would give some kind of a unified way to managing agents in the industry to charge - base their fees on a charge out rate, and a code of practice [for] what they have to do. I would legislate that landlords and tenants, or tenants associations would have to give the managing agent a job specification which is clearly defined, and carries an appropriate fee ... if there were clearer contracts, there'd be no misunderstandings."
(Managing agent, Paddington)

6.5 Overview

This chapter has reviewed a number of issues that relate to leaseholding in general, and the management of leasehold properties, in particular. Four primary issues arise. First, tenants rarely have a full understanding of the concept of 'leasehold' and its implications. Second, leases were said to be written in such a way as to give rise to difficulties with implementation and interpretation. The effect of this is, in some cases, to raise the expectations on the part of leaseholders as to the nature of the landlord's duties. It also allows the unscrupulous managing agents and landlords to evade their duties. Third, where respondents wished to take action against the managing agent or landlord most found it difficult to ascertain their rights. Fourth, while some people had considered the option of taking court action to resolve a dispute, there was a considerable body of opinion that indicated that this was not the most appropriate way of solving problems. While tenants were reluctant to take legal action for a number of reasons, the issue of cost was the primary reason for not pursuing this course of action. Finally, there was a general view, primarily from tenants and advisors, that some of the disputes that arise over leasehold management could occur because the property management profession practices without formal guidelines or controls. While the issue of professional recognition and registration was controversial, there was a considerable body of opinion that indicated that property management should be controlled in some way.

Appendices

A. Commencement dates of the Landlord and Tenant Act, 1987

B. Research Design and Conduct of the Study

C. Stage I Household screening questionnaire

D. Topic Guides

E. Group discussion display boards (Stage I)

F. Approach letter

Commencement Dates of the Landlord and Tenant Act, 1987

The Landlord and Tenant Act 1987 was implemented in a number of stages. The commencement dates are given below:

1st February 1988

> **Part I** which gives tenants of flats a right of first refusal to enable them to negotiate collectively for the purchase of the block when the landlord wishes to sell.

> **Part VI** which requires all landlords to put the name and address on all rent and service charge demands and to give an address in England, and Wales for the service of notices. It also provides for tenants to search the proprietorship register at the Land Registry for their landlord's name and address.

> **Section 45** extends the permissible objects of housing associations to enable them to manage leasehold residential property.

18th April 1988

> **Part II** which provides a procedure for tenants of flats to ask the county court to appoint a manager where the block has been neglected, thus removing the management (but not the ownership) of the block from the landlord's control.

> **Part III** gives a right of compulsory acquisition for a majority of long leaseholders, in blocks which are wholly or mainly let on long leases to apply to the court collectively to buy out the landlord's interest where the court is satisfied that he has failed in his duties and the appointment of a manager (Part II) would not be an adequate remedy.

> **Part IV** provides a mechanism for the landlord or the tenants of flats to ask the court to vary defective long leases and for a large majority to seek a variation affecting the block as a whole. There is also provision for the variation of a long lease of other dwellings as regards insurance provisions.

1st September 1988

> *Section 41* which strengthens the existing service charge provisions in the Landlord and Tenant Act 1985 and extends service charges. It entitles tenants to more information about costs incurred and gives new rights to recognised tenants' associations when a landlord wishes to carry out works.

> *Section 43* which gives tenants rights to request information about the insurance arrangements, to inspect the policy and accounts and receipts, and to challenge the level of the premium or the cover provided on the grounds

that it is unreasonable. It also enables a tenant to persuade a reluctant landlord to submit a claim or, if necessary, take other action to enable a claim to be made.

Section 44 which gives recognised tenants' associations a right to be consulted about the appointment or performance of a managing agent and to be consulted about the appointment periodically thereafter.

Under the Service Charge (Estimates and Consultation) Order 1988 the prescribed amounts above which a landlord must consult tenants about works were raised to £1,000, or £50 per dwelling.

1st April 1989

Section 42 which provides the any contributions to service charges (including sinking funds) are to be held in a trust for the benefit of the tenants. This should safeguard the funds against mis-appropriation or the landlord's insolvency.

Under a separate order - the Service charge Contributions (Authorised Investments) Order 1988 - rules concerning the investment of service charge funds held in trust (under section 42 (5) of the 1987 Act) were also implemented.

G

Research, Design and Conduct of the Study

Design, sampling and conduct of the study
The design and composition of the study

The sample was purposively selected and designed to cover a range of different types of respondents, properties and geographical locations.

Locations and types of properties

Initial consultations had indicated that usage of the 1987 Act's provisions was relatively infrequent although this varied according to geographical location. At the outset of the study it was decided to select four study areas in England, two of which were considered to be 'active', and two 'inactive' in terms of the number of enquiries about the Landlord and Tenant Act 1987 that the Department of the Environment had received.

In addition, it was important to select a range of properties, including mansion blocks, newer purpose-built blocks of flats built for owner occupation, and converted flats. Although leasehold houses were originally included in the study design, because the Act is of primary importance to occupiers of flats, these were subsequently dropped from the design.

The locations were determined by two factors: the identification of 'active' areas (in terms of the 1987 Act) through Departmental records; and the existence of a suitable range of leasehold and rented properties, identified by contacting local authorities and housing advice agencies in those areas.

The areas subsequently selected for inclusion in the study were Paddington (London), Brighton ('active' areas), Croydon, and Manchester ('inactive' areas).

Respondents

Across the two stages of the study, the sample was designed to cover four groups of people:

    i. tenants of flats who were either renting or owned a lease;

    ii. landlords of leasehold or rented flats;

    iii. agents who managed residential properties on behalf of landlords where their primary interest was in leasehold properties, rather than residential letting;

    iv. professionals who had experience of the 1987 Act, either in an advisory capacity, such as housing advisors, or had made ues of the Act's provisions (e.g. solicitors) on another person's behalf.

Tenants were selected on the basis of five quota variables:

    age
    sex
    type of tenancy

size of accommodation and
type of property.

Managing agents and landlords were selected, where possible, to give a broad spread of property portfolios.

Contact and approach
Stage one

Following visits to each of the four selected areas individual streets of properties relevant to the study were identified. Targeting the fieldwork in this way allowed a more efficient and cost-effective use of the fieldwork resources. In order to ensure that tenants met the quotas set a household screening questionnaire was used prior to inviting tenants to take part in a group discussion. In order to ensure a wide spread of respondents and properties, a maximum of two tenants per group discussion were recruited from the same block of flats. It was important that respondents should have reasonable experience of being a tenant (either renting or leasing) in their present accommodation. People with tenancies of less than 9 months were, therefore, excluded from the study. A copy of this questionnaire is shown in AppendixC.

In addition to exploring respondents' awareness and understanding of the 1987 Act, stage one of the study had two further aims. First, tenants taking part in stage one of the study who had used or had considered using the Act could be identified for follow-up in stage 2. In addition, it allowed the opportunity to identify and contact managing agents and landlords where tenants gave their permission for this to occur.

Stage two

Only a small number of tenants (4), managing agents (2), and landlords (1) were identified in stage one of the study for follow up in stage two.

A number of additional methods of tracing 'users' or 'potential users' of the Act were employed. These included approaching housing advisors, housing rights groups and solicitors in the study areas to seek their assistance in contacting people, on our behalf, who were eligible for stage two of the study. In addition, a selection of people who had written to the Department of the Environment to seek housing information were contacted. In each case, an approach letter was sent out by the Department, on our behalf. A copy of a typical approach letter is shown in Appendix F.

In tracing tenants who had used the Act we were dependent, to some extent, on advisors and solicitors in the study areas being able to provide suitable contacts. We were not able to trace any tenants who had used the Act in the Croydon study area. The stage two sample was confined primarily to the two 'active' areas, Paddington and Brighton, where usage was found to be most frequent.

Landlords were particularly difficult to trace and interview. A mail shot using 'Yellow Pages' yielded a small number of relevant landlords and managing agents; the appearance of a landlord in the Estate Gazette yielded one successful interview. Most, however, were traced through tenants, advisors and solicitors taking part in the study. Many landlords and managing agents were wary of taking part in the research. Some refused to take part; in other instances, repeated letters and telephone calls were required before an interview could be arranged.

Record type of building

Purpose-built newer block*
Purpose-built older block* (mansion block)
Converted house*
Single family house

(*IMPORTANT - BEFORE RECRUITING AT THE BUILDING CHECK THAT THERE ARE <u>THREE OR MORE</u> FLATS IN THE BLOCK (<u>EXCLUDE</u> IF ONLY ONE OR TWO FLATS IN BUILDING - IF IN DOUBT ASK RESIDENTS)

I am calling on behalf of Social and Community Planning Research, an independent social research institute. We have been asked by the DoE (Department of the Environment) to do some research looking at people's experience of being a tenant or leaseholder. We would like to invite some people to take part in the research, but first we need to ask a few questions to make sure that we talk to a good cross-section of people. Can I speak to the person in your household who has the most to do with the landlord or managing agent, for example paying rent and arranging for repairs to be carried out.

1.   How long have you lived in this flat/house?

Less than one year	1 → CLOSE
One or more years	2 → Q.2

2.   How many bedrooms does the flat/house have?

One or two	1 → CHECK QUOTA → Q.3
Three or more	2 → CHECK QUOTA → Q.3

NB. DOES NOT APPLY TO LEASEHOLD HOUSES BUT PLEASE ASK QUESTION ANYWAY.

3.   Are you a .... of this flat/house?
- <u>tenant</u> (do not own the property but pay rent to live there {not just ground rent})
- <u>leaseholder</u> (own the flat/house but not the land, pay ground rent to a landlord or managing agent)
- <u>freeholder</u> (own both flat/house and land, have no landlord or managing agent)

Tenant	1 → CHECK QUOTA → Q.4a
Leaseholder	2 → CHECK QUOTA → SKIP TO Q.5
Freeholder	3 → CLOSE
Don't know	4 → CLOSE

4a.   ASK TENANTS (RENTING) ONLY
Do you pay a service charge for the upkeep of the building that is <u>separate</u> from your rent? (ie the service charge is <u>not</u> included in the rent)

Yes	1 → Q.4b
No	2 → Q.4b
Don't know	3 → Q.4b

4b. ASK TENANTS (RENTING) ONLY
When did your tenancy agreement begin? Was it ....

Before 15th January 1989	1 → Q.5
On or after 15th January 1989	2 → Q.5
Don't know	3 → Q.5

5. And does this flat/house come with your job, or another member of your family's job?

Yes	1 → CLOSE
No	2 → Q.6

The next few questions are to do with landlords.
(EXPLAIN TO LEASEHOLDERS - by landlord I mean the owner of the freehold)

6. Can I check what type of landlord you have?
Is it ...

Private Landlord	1 → Q.7
Local Authority	2 → CLOSE
Housing Association	3 → CLOSE
Housing Trust	4 → CLOSE
Another charitable body	5 → CLOSE

(PROPERTIES HAVE BEEN SELECTED TO HAVE PRIVATE LANDLORDS SO THIS QUESTION IS JUST TO DOUBLE CHECK)

7. And do you yourself own the freehold of any property?

Yes	1 → CLOSE
No	2 → Q.8

8. ASK FOR FLATS/CONVERSIONS ONLY (NOT LEASEHOLD HOUSES)
Does your landlord live on the premises?

Yes	1 → Q.9a
No	2 → Q.9a

9a. We are trying to make sure that we don't talk to too many people with the same landlord or managing agent. Do you know the name of your landlord? Of your managing agent (may not apply in all cases)?

Yes	1 → Q.9b
No	2 → SKIP TO Q.10

9b. Would you mind telling me the name/s?
WRITE IN

LANDLORD _____

MANAGING AGENT _____

_____

DO NOT RECRUIT MORE THAN TWO PEOPLE PER GROUP WITH THE SAME LANDLORD/MANAGING AGENT.

10. Occupation of respondent?
    (PLEASE WRITE IN)

_____

EXCLUDE IF RESPONDENT IS   - LAWYER
                                                - SOLICITOR
                                              - ESTATE AGENT/MANAGING AGENT
                                              - INVOLVED IN PROVIDING HOUSING ADVICE

11. Age of respondent
    (PLEASE WRITE IN) _____

Under 30	1 → CHECK QUOTA
30 to 50	2 → CHECK QUOTA
Over 50	3 → CHECK QUOTA

12. Sex of respondent?

Male	1
Female	2

IF INTERVIEWEE QUALIFIES, INVITE TO ATTEND GROUP DISCUSSION. EXPLAIN THAT THE DISCUSSION WILL COVER TOPICS SUCH AS WHAT IT IS LIKE TO BE A TENANT/LEASEHOLDER WITH A PRIVATE LANDLORD, AND ANY DIFFICULTIES THAT ARISE. IF NECESSARY STRESS THAT NO PRIOR KNOWLEDGE IS NEEDED.

Please record <u>outcome</u> of all screening interviews here:

Recruited	☐
Not recruited - quotas filled	☐
Not recruited - out of quota	☐
Eligible but refused	☐

RECRUITMENT DETAILS

NAME: MR/MRS/MS/MISS _____

ADDRESS: _____

_____

_____ PHONE NO.: _____

Appendix D   Topic Guides

1.   Stage 1   Tenants

2.   Stage 1   Managing Agents and Landlords

3.   Stage 2   Tenants

4.   Stage 2   Advisers/Solicitors

5.   Stage 2   Managing Agents and Landlords

8

LANDLORD AND TENANT ACT, 1987

Phase 1

Topic guide - Tenants

1. Background

- Own accommodation
  - size
  - number in household

- The building
  - type and size
  - facilities (eg. garages, lifts)
  - variations within the building (tenancies, size of flat)
  - condition of building

- About the tenancy
  - type and length

- History of housing tenancies
  - previous experience; type of tenancy (briefly)

2. Experience of renting and leasing properties

- Contact with the managing agent/landlord
  - do they know who the managing agent/landlord is; do they have addess in the UK? - how do they know?
  - method of contact; how often
  - for what reasons do/would they contact managing agent/landlord
  - how easy

- Information/consultation
  - does the managing agent/landlord keep them informed; e.g. repairs; service charges; tenants rights, etc.
  - what information do they think they are entitled to (e.g. service charges)
  - how could they best be informed; type of information required
  - any difficulties in finding out about calculation of SERVICE CHARGES; how SERVICE CHARGE money is held
  - have they ever been consulted; what about; what did they feel about it
  - how could they best be consulted; what should they be consulted about
  - have there been occasions when they would have liked to be consulted; what about

- Payment and rent (including ground rent and service charges)
  - what do they pay (rent, ground rent, service charges); are service charges paid separately or 'inclusive' in the rent
  - what services do they receive
  - do service charges represent good value for money
  - do they know how the payments for service charges are calculated

Role of tenant/managing agent/landlord

- expectations about landlord's responsibilities
- expectations about managing agent's responsibilities
- differences between managing agents/landlords
- expectations about tenants' responsibilities
- what happens in practice
- have expectations changed since moving in

Satisfaction with managing agent/landlord

- Brief details of any problems that have arisen or outstanding
- have they ever talked to the managing agent/landlord about their problems; what happened
- has the landlord ever changed the MA because of complaints/problems

3. Dealings with the managing agent/landlord

- Have they ever taken any action against their managing agent/landlord

IF ACTION TAKEN THEN ASK

- what prompted them; what were the circumstances
- what action did they take
- how did they go about taking action; sources of information; sources of help
- what were their expectations; what happened in practice
- what was the outcome of their action

IF NO ACTION TAKEN THEN ASK

- ever thought about taking action. IF NO why not
- under what circumstances would they take action
- what action would they take
- how would they go about taking action

- Using advisors and advocates

  - have they ever taken advice for a housing problem; from whom
  - what were their expectations; what happened in practice

ASK IF NOT TAKEN ADVICE FOR A HOUSING PROBLEM

- who would they go to (reasons for not seeking professional advice)
- what would they expect to happen
- views about **availability** of housing advice and information; sources; what should be available
- views about **usefulness** of housing advice and information; what would be useful

- Tenants Association/Residents Association

  - is there a tenants/residents association

ASK IF THERE IS A TENANTS/RESIDENTS ASSOCIATION

- is the membership representative; are they a member
- does the managing agent/landlord recognise it
- have they used the Tenants/Residents Association to help resolve a problem with the managing agent/landlord over SERVICE CHARGES AND/OR INFORMATION ABOUT BUILDING WORKS; what happened; how successful; any problems

- why isn't there an association; would they like one; would they be a member
- what would they want an association to do for them, e.g. SERVICE CHARGES AND/OR INFORMATION ABOUT BUILDING WORKS; perceived advantages and disadvantages

• Views on renting versus leasing

- perceived differences
- advantages and disadvantages
- reasons for renting or leasing; contrast with reasons for being a freeholder

• Ever been offered opportunity to buy the property from the landlord (under Right of first refusal)

• Comparison with other types of landlord

- have they ever lived in different type of accommodation, e.g. freehold, rented from local authority, housing association; how did it compare, preferences; difference between landlord and managing agents

4. Awareness of housing-related legislation (Briefly)

• Are they aware of any legislation that could help them resolve any problems with the managing agent/landlord

IF SO,

- what legislation
- what rights does the legislation give them
- how useful is it to them
- how did they find out about it
- have they made use of it

IF YES

- what prompted its use
- how successful were they
- would they use it again

IF NO

- under what circumstances would they use it (Explore reasons for not using legislation)

5. Awareness and views about the Landlord and Tenant Act, 1987

• Awareness of the 1987 Act

- sources of information
- what are their rights under the Act
- what are landlords' duties under the Act

• Have they used the Act

- if they have used the Act; under what circumstances; any problems; how successful were they
- If they **have not** used the Act would they use it; under what circumstances

IF NOT AWARE OF THE ACT OR SPECIFIC RIGHTS UNDER THE ACT, PROBE EACH OF THE FOLLOWING SECTIONS IN TURN.

USE SHOW CARDS WITH SYNOPSIS OF ACT'S PROVISIONS

1 Information about the landlord
2 Service charges
3 Insurance of the property
4 Role of tenants' associations
5 Variation of leases
6 Appointment of a manager by the court
7 Compulsory acquisition
8 Right of first refusal
    PROBE whether ever experienced a landlord try to get out of this
    e.g. selling without telling tenant/getting up a company to avoid
    responsibility

For each section, PROBE

- awareness and understanding
- to whom these rights apply
- the procedures required by the Act, including the time periods required by
    the Act
- experience of using the Act (if not already covered)
- usefulness or potential usefulness of the Act's provision
- would/did the Act's provisions solve **their** problems; what would solve
    their problems
- would they use the Act; why not
- in what circumstances would they use the Act

- Who do they think the Act benefits

- (Generally) does the Act seem useful to them; why/why not

- For people who rent/lease what legislation, guidelines or regulations would they
  like to see

  - how could managing agents/landlords be regulated/made accountable

- Is there sufficient information available about housing legislation; what should
  be available; what format should it be in.

LANDLORD AND TENANT ACT, 1987

Phase 1

Topic guide - Managing agents and landlords

1. Background

- Buildings owned/managed; location; size; type

- Types of tenancies

2. Role and Responsibilities of managing agents/landlords

ASK LANDLORDS THAT MANAGE AND MANAGING AGENTS

- Role and managerial responsibilities, e.g. property maintenance, services, other aspects
    - role of managing agent
    - role of landlord; why do they manage rather than assign to managing agent
    - role of landlord where there is also a managing agent
    - how do landlords feel about MAs and MAs about landlords
    - does managerial role vary according to the style of
        i. property, in terms of age, size, type
        ii. tenancy; renting or leasing

ASK NON-MANAGING LANDLORDS

- why don't they manage
- benefits/disadvantages of using a managing agent
- their view of managing agents role and their role

ASK ALL

- Difficulties arising from being a managing agent/landlord
    - dealings with tenants
    - dealing with Tenants/Residents Associations
    - accounting procedures (in respect of SERVICE CHARGES)

ASK ALL LANDLORDS

- Reasons for property ownership
eg. investment potential/rental income/investment interest from service charge monies held in Trust; which is the most important
    - Does this affect the way the building is managed - priorities

3. Dealing with tenants

- Dealing with tenants
    - how much contact do they have; what sort of contact
    - when would they contact tenants eg. collecting rent; to see if satisfied; repairs and maintenance
    - any problems dealing with tenants
    - how do they see tenants
    - how do they feel about their relations with tenants could they be improved; how

H

- Dealing with Tenants/Residents Associations
  - are there any TA's in any buildings they manage
  - should there be a TA (if appropriate)
  - role of TA - knowledge of legal obligations to TA (consultation over appointment of MA, building works, etc.)
  - do they recognise the TA; why/why not
  - how much contact do they have; what sort of contact
  - when would they contact the TA (inc. legal obligations if not already covered)
  - issues raised by TA; what was the last issue raised
  - any problems when dealing with TAs
  - (landlords) how do they feel about consulting TAs over appointment of MA; do they take tenants' views into account; have they ever changed MAs because of tenants' views
  - how do they feel about their relations with TAs; could they be improved; how

- Providing information/consultation
  - do they provide any information to their tenants (eg tenants rights, service charges, repairs, costs); why/why not; what sort; what form is it in
  - what are they legally obliged to provide
  - are they happy with the information they provide
  - difficulties in providing information (particularly accounting procedures for SERVICE CHARGES)
  - benefits/disadvantages of providing information to tenants
  - how do tenants feel about the information they provide (if known)
  - do tenants ask for information; what sort; can/do they provide; how do they provide
  - when would they consult their tenants; repairs; insurance; appointment of managing agent

- Service charges
  - how are they held; accounting procedures; difficulties
  - information provided to tenants; how much; in what form; in response to request

PROBE knowledge of legal requirements

- Varying the lease
  - if the tenants wanted to vary the lease (over repairs, maintenance, provision of services, building's insurance, and calculation of service charges) what would they do

PROBE awareness of legal requirements and tenants' rights

- Management of the property
  - if the tenants expressed a dislike of the way the property was being managed, what would they do

PROBE awareness of legal requirements and tenants' rights

104

- Selling the property

    - if they wanted to sell the property would they inform the tenants (knowledge of legal requirements); what information would they give
    - (any) experience of selling a tenanted property since 1988; what happened
    - would they buy a property where right of first refusal not given; knowledge of legal consequences (any knowledge/experience of landlords trying to avoid right of first refusal)

PROBE awareness of legal requirements and tenants' rights

    - what happens to SERVICE CHARGE money

4. Awareness of Landlord and Tenant Act, 1987

- Experience of legislation

    - has any legislation been used by tenants against them; what was it; under what circumstances

- Awareness of the 1987 Act

    - sources of information
    - what are the major changes that have been introduced
    - what are tenants' rights under the Act
    - what are landlord's duties under the Act

IF NOT ALREADY COVERED - has the 1987 Act been used against them; under what circumstances; what happened

IF NOT AWARE OF THE ACT OR SPECIFIC RIGHTS UNDER THE ACT, PROBE EACH OF THE FOLLOWING SECTIONS IN TURN

USE INFORMATION CARDS WITH SYNOPSIS OF PROVISIONS

1 Information about the landlord
2 Service charges
3 Insurance of the property
4 Role of tenants' associations
5 Variation of leases
6 Appointment of a manager by the court
7 Compulsory acquisition
8 Right of first refusal

For each section, PROBE

    - awareness and understanding
    - to whom these rights apply
    - experience of the Act; perceived barriers to use by tenants
    - the procedures required by the Act, including the time periods required by the Act
    - experience of using the Act
    - fairness of the Act
    - how does it effect tenants
    - how does it effect managing agent/landlords

- Who do they think the Act benefits

- (Generally) How effectively does the Act ensure tenants' rights

- How does the Act change landlord/managing agent's practices

- What legislation, regulations or guidelines should there be to ensure a beneficial relationship between landlords/managing agents and tenants.

LANDLORD AND TENANT ACT 1987

Phase 2

Topic Guide - Advisers/Solicitors etc.

1. **Brief description of organisation**
   - affiliation/funding
   - aims and objectives/specialisms

2. **Respondents background and role in organisation**

3. **Profile of "housing" clients**
   - main types of problems
   - expectations from agency
   - where referred from

   Prompt - leases
     - service charges
     - buying freehold
     - managing agent

   [ADVISERS ONLY]

4. **Awareness of recent legislation**
   - do with landlords/tenants

5. **Awareness of 1987 Act**
   - how detailed
   - where from/in what form

   [ADVISERS AND SOLICITORS]

6. **Experiences of advising/asking for tenants**
   - examples of circumstances and issues/problems (which are the most common)
   - what happened   - what did they do
                      - what did tenants do
                      - what did landlord/managing agent do
   - what was the outcome
   - if legal action was taken - which part(s) of the Act
       was the procedure satisfactory? Why? Why not?
       was the outcome satisfactory? Why? Why not?
   - if legal action was not taken, why not?
   - what would make the process easier/more effective?

7. Assessment of 1987 Act

What are their views about the scope and effectiveness of the 1987 Landlord and Tenant Act?

USE CARDS TO GO THROUGH PROVISIONS OF THE ACT

1 Information about the landlord
2 Service charges
3 Insurance of the property
4 Role of tenants' associations
5 Variation of leases
6 Appointment of a manager by the court
7 Compulsory acquisition
8 Right of first refusal (probe whether experience of a landlord trying to get out of this ... eg. selling without telling/setting up company to avoid responsibility).

Probe for -   client awareness
           -   usefulness (to whom?)
           -   relevance to client problems
           -   advice sought/given
           -   loopholes
           -   suggestions for change

8. Overall Evaluation

Are there any gaps: ie issues not covered by the Act/legislation? What are they?

What guidelines/legislation/regulation would they like to see for people who rent/lease? (PROBE FOR FEELINGS ABOUT GOING TO COURT ETC.)

Do they think leaseholders fully understand what leaseholding involves prior to purchase? How well do people know/understand their leases?

Any suggestions concerning the format or language of leases.

Is there sufficient information available about housing legislation? What would be available? What form should it be in?

Whose role is it to interpret/publicise legislation? eg. Managing Agent, landlord, solicitor etc.?

LANDLORD AND TENANT ACT 1987

Phase 2

Topic Guide - Tenants

1. Background

Own flat - number of beds etc

Type and size of building (number of units)

Age of property

Condition

Shared facilities/common parts

Tenancy - type and length (eg. rented or leasehold)

Management of building - landlord/managing agent/management company

Responsibilities   -   what is tenant responsible for (under lease)
                    -   what is landlord/managing agent/management company respo:

2. Contact with landlord/managing agent

Do they have name and UK address for landlord

Who tends to do the contacting; how often; about what; method

How easy is access

3. Seeking advice/taking action

Are there any issues/problems which have arisen in their tenancy for which they have sought advice or taken action

- what kind of issue (describe)
- who did they consult. Why?, How found?
- were they aware of their legal rights/appropriate legislation - what happened?
- did they consider/take legal action, what was the outcome?
- if they did not take legal action, why not?
- was the procedure satisfactory - why; why not?
- was the outcome satisfactory why, why not?
- what would have made the process easier/more effective?

4. Overall evaluation

Check for awareness of the Act itself ... if took legal action, were they aware of the particular legislation used?

Are there any gaps: ie issues not covered by the Act/legislation? What are they?

What guidelines/legislation/regulation would they like to see for people who rent/lease? (PROBE FOR FEELINGS ABOUT GOING TO COURT ETC.)

Do they think leaseholders fully understand what leaseholding involves prior to purchase? How well do people know/understand their leases?

Any suggestions concerning the format or language of leases.

Is there sufficient information available about housing legislation? What should be available? What form should it be in?

Whose role is it to interpret/publicise legislation? eg. Managing Agent, landlord, solicitor etc.?

LANDLORD AND TENANT ACT, 1987

Phase 2

Topic guide - Managing agents and landlords

1. Background

- Buildings owned/managed; location; size; type

- Types of tenancies

2. Awareness of Landlord and Tenant Act, 1987

- Awareness of the 1987 Act

  - sources of information
  - what are the major changes that have been introduced
  - what are tenants' rights under the Act
  - what are landlords' duties under the Act

3. Experience of the Landlord and Tenant Act, 1987

- Have they ever used the Act, eg. Right of first refusal; variation of leases

  - under what circumstances have they used it
  - what happened; what did they do ; what did tenants do
  - what was the outcome
  - if legal action was taken; which part(s) of the Act; was the procedure satisfactory; was the outcome satisfactory
  - if legal action was not taken; why not?
  - what would make the process easier/more effective

- When would they use the Act?

- Have they ever had the Act used against them?

  - under what circumstances
  - what happened; what did tenants do; what did they do
  - what was the outcome
  - if legal action was taken; which part(s) of the Act; was the procedure satisfactory; was the outcome satisfactory?
  - what would make the process easier/more effective

Assessment of 1987 Act

What are their views about the scope and effectiveness of the 1987 Landlord and Tenant Act?

USE CARDS TO GO THROUGH PROVISIONS OF THE ACT.

1 Information about the landlord
2 Service charges
3 Insurance of the property
4 Role of tenants' associations
5 Variation of leases
6 Appointment of a manager by the court
7 Compulsory acquisition
8 Right of first refusal (probe whether experience of a landlord trying to get out of this .... eg. selling without telling/setting up company to avoid responsibility)

Probe for - client awareness
           - usefulness (to whom?)
           - relevance to client problems
           - advice sought/given
           - loopholes
           - suggestions for change

5. Overall Evaluation   Are there any gaps: ie. issues not covered by the Act/legislation? What are they?

What guidelines/legislation/regulation would they like to see for people who rent/lease. (Probe for feelings about going to court, etc.)

Do they think leaseholders fully understand what leaseholding involves prior to purchase? How well do people know/understand their leases?

Any suggestions concerning the format or language of leases.

Is there sufficient information available about housing legislation?

What should be available? What form should it be in?

Whose role is it to interpret/publicise legislation? eg. Managing Agent, landlord, solicitor, etc.?

Group Discussion Display Boards (Phase 1)

1. Information about the Landlord

Tenants and leaseholders have a right to know the name of their landlord and a contact address in England and Wales.

Tenants and leaseholders are entitled to search Land Registry records to find out their landlord's name and address.

Any demands for payment (eg rent or service charges) must contain the landlord's name and contact address.

2. Service Charges

Tenants and leaseholders have a right to know how the service charge is calculated, to inspect receipts and to challenge sums demanded.

Tenants and leaseholders are entitled to be consulted about building works, to see estimates and to challenge the standards of work, the cost, or the amount of advance payments demanded.

Service charge payments must be held in trust by the landlord or managing agent.

3. Insurance of the property

Tenants and leaseholders are entitled to know about the insurance cover for their property and to challenge the landlord's choice.

They have the right to know:

- the name of the insurer
- the amount insured
- what the policy covers

4. Role of Tenants Associations (Residents Associations)

Tenants Associations have the right to be consulted over the appointment of managing agents who run the property on behalf of the landlord.

Tenants Associations should be consulted over any major works to be carried out. They are entitled to receive detailed specifications of the work and to obtain their own estimates.

5. Variation of leases

Landlords or leaseholders with long leases (more than 21 years) can apply to have aspects of their lease changed where provisions are considered unsatisfactory in relation to:

- repairs or maintenance of the building or of particular safety or security installations
- provision of services (eg. cleaning)
- building insurance
- calculation of service charges and the recovery of other expenditure incurred

Leases have to be seriously "defective" before they can be re-written, and amendments then apply collectively (to all the other leaseholders in the property)

6. Appointment of a manager by the court

Tenants and leaseholders (of flats) can apply to the court to have a manager or receiver appointed where the landlord or managing agent does not carry out his/her legal obligations properly (eg. in terms of repairs or maintenance).

An application is made where the landlord is thought unlikely to put matters right of his/her own accord.

7. Compulsory acquisition

In extreme cases where a landlord has failed to meet his/her obligations, and where a manager or receiver has already been appointed, tenants and leaseholders can apply to the court to acquire the property from the landlord.

8. Right of first refusal

If a landlord intends to sell a property, qualifying tenants and leaseholders (of flats) have the right of first refusal: the property must first be offered to them.

Tenants and leaseholders can then decide whether to negotiate (collectively) to buy the property or to refuse the offer.

If the landlord sells without giving the tenants the right of first refusal, they can obtain details of the sale from the new landlord and serve a purchase notice on him/her.

Appendix F   Approach Letters

DEPARTMENT OF THE ENVIRONMENT LETTER

To Whom it May Concern

The Department of Environment have asked SCPR (Social and Community Planning Research) to carry out a study amongst landlords, managing agents and tenants. The purpose of the study is to identify any problems or difficulties which they have and to hear about their opinion of relevant legislation and any experience they have with using it.

I do hope that you will agree to participate in the study. If you would like to discuss it further, I can be contacted on the above number.

Yours sincerely

Mrs Margaret Thomas
Social Research Division

SOCIAL AND COMMUNITY PLANNING RESEARCH LETTER

Evaluation of Landlord and Tenant Act, 1987

The Department of the Environment has commissioned a research study to evaluate the above legislation. The research is being carried out by Social and Community Planning Research (SCPR), an independent research institute.

The purpose of the research is to look at any issues or problems which may arise in the management of residential property from both the landlords' and tenants' point of view and in particular, in relation to the Landlord and Tenant Act, 1987.

We are very interested in your experience and opinions of this piece of legislation and its relevance and usefulness in dealing with landlord – tenant issues. We would very much like to talk either you or the person in your organisation who is likely to be familiar with the legislation and hope that we may arrange an interview at a convenient time.

May we stress that any information you give in the interview will be treated in the strictest confidence, and will only be used for the purposes of the research.

We would be very grateful for your help and will telephone you soon to answer any questions that you may have about the study, and to see whether you would be interested in taking part.

Yours sincerely

Andrew Thomas
Cathy North
Liz Spencer
Kit Ward
Qualitative Research Unit

Printed in the United Kingdom by HMSO at Edinburgh Press
Dd 293991 C20 8/91 (292090)